Just a Girl Who Loves the Beatles

A Memoir—My Fab Four Fun Through the Years

Lana Lozito

ISBN 978-1-09833-217-4 (print)
ISBN: 978-1-09833-218-1 (ebook)

Disclaimer
This book is a memoir. It reflects the author's
present recollections of experiences over time. Some
names and characteristics have been changed, some
events have been compressed, and some dialogues have
been recreated.

Cover designed by Maria Siragusa

Printed in the United States of America

First Edition

Follow on Instagram @ justagirlwholovestheBeatles

*Dedicated to the sweet memory of
Mrs. Louise Harrison—a caring, kindred
spirit to Beatles fans everywhere.*

"Memories are but a journey we take in our minds, but relive in our hearts."

—A. Grant

CONTENTS

Postmarked from WOOLTON, LIVERPOOL —1965

"Love to Lana
Louise Harrison"

INTRODUCTION

Are you someone who happens to see the name Beatles and then pauses for a brief second glance? You might be just breezing through a magazine and see something written about one of the Beatles or all four of them from back in the day. How about a talk show on TV where Paul or Ringo are appearing? Don't touch that remote! Or, as I like to remember, "Don't touch that dial!"—you wouldn't dare switch over to something else. You still want to see the Beatles, still want to hear what they say, and still want to know anything you can. Just that fleeting moment of being reconnected to them makes you sit up and take notice.

I am one of those people; I have always been hooked. I love to recall the times that have passed if it is Beatles-related. I am especially captivated when I hear one of their songs. I can certainly remember when that particular song entered my life and I begin to feel the vibe of that moment all over again. I take delight in the emotions attached to these memories and know that what's deep inside never changes; my Beatles memories remain a part of me to enjoy, explore, and discover in brand-new ways. There is no expiration date on Fab Four fun.

How did I think I could write a story? Me? A writer? High school essays were a major chore for me; term papers, a nerve-ravaged struggle. Creative writing was totally out of my comfort zone. All of a sudden, though, I found myself filled with excitement, and that tingle gave me the motivation and enthusiasm to tackle a project such as this. Debbie, a dearest and oldest friend, calls this feeling being "inspired."

My greatest inspiration came from my collection of letters from Mrs. Louise Harrison. Yes! I am in possession of approximately four years of correspondence with George Harrison's mother. These letters are my personal treasures of back and forth with her and something that kept me smiling through most of my teen years. Throughout, her letters proved she had been one of the most ardent of Beatles fans as well as a loving "mum"; her sweetness was very apparent in all that was the George we idolized. After over fifty years of conserving these precious notes, I knew I wanted to keep the thoughts of her letters alive. I realized it was all part of the fun in my youth, and it was also obvious the Beatles were behind it all. Her letters and notes always left me astonished as they have stayed the course in the entirety of my Beatles journey. As I share bits of her letters as lighthearted intros to each chapter, it feels like I am keeping her a lasting memory of kindness and love.

Along with the letters she often sent items like a picture postcard or a small foldout "Pixerama" photo book of the group in their early days. This booklet was published in 1963, a year before we in America knew them. She signed it: *Love to Lana, Louise Harrison*. When I received it, I curiously unfolded each photo slowly and carefully in awe. I treasured her unique little Beatles gift and appreciated her thoughtfulness. It made me feel rather special.

As the letters continued, I began to thoroughly enjoy the casual and friendly bond with her as she put a few words to a piece of paper that would eventually find its way from her Liverpool home to my mailbox in Lynbrook, NY. Those letters were also my connection to something that was unobtainable—the Beatles were unobtainable. Being your average Beatlemaniac in those days, I could only hope for a personal link to them. After many years, though, I realized that having that relationship with George's mum was my particular connection.

How was it even possible that my life was so Beatles-infused over the past fifty odd years? I decided I would put it all down if only for me to indulge my silliness. I could read my story over and over again and share with Debbie those moments of innocence and pleasure. I would be a teenager all over again and would relive the pure joy of being "just a girl who loves the Beatles." The music and the mania are happily my keepsakes forever; there is nothing or no one that could take that away.

In the mid-1960s, Debbie and I lived around the corner from each other and would meet many a morning to take that mile-long walk to school. We would

be chatting nonstop all the way, and the topic of
our conversations would be only the Beatles. We were
totally consumed by the intensity of it all: what
the Beatles did, what they said, what they sang, or
which magazine had written news about them or posted
pictures of them. This was our life, our waking
thoughts, our nighttime dreams, our hopes to know
more about these amazing four guys, and our fears
that we might miss something they did or said. We
were friends then and are friends today. Even now
during our daily routine telephonic coffee klatch,
we often use "remember" when talking about the Fab
Four. This is always fun, but at this point in my
life, I want to celebrate those innermost feelings
of long ago, knowing well that those sentiments have
always been heartfelt.

Their music grabbed my soul and wouldn't let go.
Their harmonies were addicting, their words had more
than rhyme and reason, and the melodies were hypno-
tizing. Undeniably, I had grown very fond of these
four lads and their sound. I remember spending many
afternoons relaxing on the black sectional sofa in
my living room, staring at the front of my *Meet the
Beatles!* LP cover, then reading and rereading every
word on the back cover while, of course, listening to every track. Their songs filled the room and
beyond; *Meet the Beatles!* music continued to play
for hours—over and over and over again. That mono LP
was my first recording of theirs and had become my
very own mantra; I was forever in a Beatles trance.

Once I was drawn into any Beatles song, the lyrics,
all of a sudden, would be instantly memorized without
even realizing I had such a talent; it was quiescent
magic. I could sing along with them word for word on

any given tune. It became enlightening to learn about love and life through their words. Their songs were more than poetry put to music, touching your heart in every way. If only I could memorize poems in English Lit that quick. Why was that? Why on earth had those four lads been such an influence in my life and on countless others'? What was their charm? Maybe there was something lacking in my life, creating a void that needed to be filled, or maybe their charisma touched me in a way that I could never imagine, or their funny comments and accents were something so new and unlike anything I had ever experienced up until that time, or, oh yes, I need to mention, maybe they were just too adorable—plain and simple.

Today, one just has to get on YouTube to find any video clip ever taken or any word ever spoken in an interview or any song ever sung by John, Paul, George, or Ringo. That internet link will bring you to another and yet another and you will be well educated on every detail about them. There will never be that moment of missing something; it is all there to view and listen. I am always thrilled to learn something new about them; it makes me feel like the first time I read the British fanzine *Beatles Monthly* and walked through the secret passages into their lives. Even on Facebook and Instagram there are posts by Paul and Ringo along with the families of George and John reminding us of Beatles history, a birthday celebration or special occasion with music videos and rare photos. They embrace social media and keep the Beatles magic fresh and alive. Then there is the glory of the Beatles channel on Sirius XM Radio, which offers you nonstop music, stories, and bits of their many interviews that will make your ride even more pleasurable. This Beatles station dissects the science of the group. The broadcasters clearly reveal the pure methodology of their music and decipher every lyric ever written by them; for that brief period, I am truly in the '60's moment. It is especially moving to listen to the common thread among the fans and other musicians showing their love and admiration for the Fab Four.

It is quite obvious that the sentimentality of Beatlemania has taken on a life of its own and continues to grow and grow. The mania for the Beatles was electrifying and has proven to be everlasting. We can never get too much of the hype about them. The "Baby Boomer" generation (of which I am a part) has discovered a mystical fountain of youth through the Beatles. We embrace it. All we needed was love and we definitely found it in their legacy.

The afterlife of the Fab Four brought forward many authorized and unauthorized biographies of them as a group and as individuals. Some are very in-depth, tell-all books about their personal lives and, honestly, at times not an easy read. Many representations are of their rough times and yes, they are human; but I refuse to dwell on anything negative about them. It will always be their music and evident charm that would forever keep me in a place Deb would rightly call a "Beatles Bubble."

The trips down memory lane are insightful, but for me, they cannot compare to my personal spiritual journey with the Beatles. For me, their musical notes and lyrics are therapeutic techniques for always getting that feel-good sentiment at any point in time. It is definitely the cure-all for anything that is ailing you. Their sound has always transported me to a safe place to linger; it is my cozy hideaway. I can always turn to their music and message for that smile and sweet sigh.

This is love; I think I found the real thing.

Postmarked from WOOLTON, LIVERPOOL '25—3 AU 65

"Paul received your letter but as he gets 1,000s he asked me to send you a reply."

Chapter 1

1964 AB *(AFTER BEATLES)*

———————

For any young girl in 1964 AB, life would never be the same. Of course, over time some got over the Beatlemania phase, but others did not. I am here to talk about those who kept the impact of the Beatles close in mind and heart. How we all dealt with these four young lads and what they had to say and sing would leave a permanent soft spot in our soul. Volumes have been written on the effect the mop tops had on America and the world after they appeared on *The Ed Sullivan Show*, that famous Sunday night in February. That one night would go on to be a game changer in the lives of so many, me included. It was definitely a cultural revolution as it has been written, but in my case, it was just plain innocent fun. As I moved out from tween to well into my early teen years, the Beatles seemed to be my rite of passage into the beginning of my independence. I was all of a sudden an official teenager with my own thoughts and ideas, my own direction, and my own happy times. All of a sudden, I was having my own fun of bubbly giddiness, and smile-on-my-face excitement—the Beatles did this.

1964 BB *(Before Beatles)* was a time during which music was always a part of my life. There was always some tune echoing in our house. My parents enjoyed playing records from their '40's era and were also very into the popular music of the '50s and '60s. My brother and I were thrilled when they purchased our first stereo suitcase record player with detachable speakers. They also bought some funky looking orange vinyl LPs in stereo to accompany the new player. Imagine the first experience of deciphering a record played in stereo. It was incredible listening to something coming out of one speaker and yet another part of the song coming out of the other; it definitely felt futuristic and "new age."

My older brother was fanatical about his rock and roll music of the '50s and early '60s, which I loved, too. His collection of 45s was extensive, and he played those sounds whenever he could share the record player. How I loved his favorite music of Motown, Chuck Berry, Gary U.S. Bonds, The Ronettes, and especially The Everly Brothers (not knowing then how that Everly harmonizing sound would grab me once again, but more profoundly the second time with the Fab Four). I would dance around the house to any tune he played and have a blast. I moved from room to room to *Quarter to Three* like I was on the dance floor in those lyrics. Those sounds were his time, though, his nostalgia to be. Then it was my turn. It was the era that would be known to me as AB *(After Beatles)*, and everything was brand new. Music had changed into something completely unrecognizable and it took me totally by surprise. Those days in early 1964 AB, Beatlemania had its first beginnings in the States; the passion of "intense fan frenzy" was a curious sensation and a bit overwhelming—all in a fun way.

And, so it began. Their music belonged to me and I was never letting go, but it was more than the music; they were so much more. I felt close to them more as friends than musical idols. They gave countless interviews, and watching those I learned about their personalities little by little. Whenever I watched them speak, I felt cozy, as they were all about their funny, friendly demeanor and their down-to-earth manner. It was certainly the key to the comfort I felt. They were a positive influence and my new buddies. I was forever faithful to that connection.

I read any and every magazine story I could find about them. I also began reading the daily newspaper on a regular basis just to search for any article written about them, which were many. I knew exactly where to check in the "Entertainment" section and find a sentence here and there. I clipped any photo or word about them and created a scrapbook. It was a sweet moment when I could add a new item to my book. I would then sit back, get comfortable, and open each page slowly from the beginning to ponder and enjoy.

Friendships at that time revolved around which one of the Beatles you were in love with. There was Jane, who loved George, Ann loved John, Debbie loved Paul, and Linda loved Ringo. At the onset of Beatlemania, I was a Paul lover because, well, come on, he was so perfectly cute. In one of my first letters to Mrs. Harrison, I asked her to pass along a letter to Paul. I also sent a favorite photo I had of him and asked her to have Paul sign it. She replied and returned my photo with a very noticeable Paul McCartney signature scribbled on the bottom right corner of the pic. I cannot verify or claim it is truly his signature, but she made me very happy that day.

Over the years some of my feelings changed, though, and I started to realize what my good buddy Jane knew all along, George was the man. Of course, I still loved dear, gorgeous Paul, but also discovered a little more of George to grab my heart. George was always portrayed as the "Quiet Beatle," but over time, the only characteristic about him that remained constant was that he was the nice one. I was especially drawn to his humor and uncanny wit. The other three had a real talent for this, but for me George was the master. Yes, in 1964, my "I Love Paul" button was firmly affixed to my pocketbook, but I was only thirteen years old. What did I know? George was someone to learn more about and be happily surprised. He was a deep, spiritual, kind soul that simply took your breath away.

I was fortunate to get my hands on a six-foot colored poster of the Beatles in one of their classic poses, dressed in the famous collarless suit by the London-based tailor, Douglas Millings. I immediately scotch-taped that poster to my bedroom door and continually glanced over at it while my transistor radio played on throughout the day waiting for a Beatles song. That poster certainly consumed the whole room and that was just fine by me, and only me. I can still see my dad roll his eyes each time he walked down the hallway and passed my room.

As I started my collections of Beatles cards, I became totally engaged in trying to get complete sets, leaving me with an innumerable amount of doubles and way too much pink bubble gum. After a few series of black-and-white cards, Topps issued a series of photo cards in color, and I became totally engrossed in the details on the back of these cards showing a question-and-answer dialogue. It was just another connection with each individual Beatle, and I could get another intimate look into their likes and lives. This was more than fun; I was getting closer and closer to them with each little snapshot interview.

I joined the "Official Beatles Fan Club" because I could get my hands on the newsletters with the happenings and other personal information about the Beatles I could eagerly devour. Those Christmas greetings from the Fab Four each year were especially creative. I distinctly remember the black cardboard paper record I received one year. It was their fourth Christmas record called *Everywhere It's Christmas*. What a fun recording of them laughing, telling stories, and joking around. I also remember another recording of their holiday wishes to the fans called *The Beatles - Happy Christmas, Happy New Year*. Wasn't it "Merry Christmas?" Oh really, that's how they say it in England? This was interesting; I loved learning all the little details of what made them who they were. Another year the fan club sent out a beautiful black-and-white photo card with holiday greetings, which I framed and still put out on display each and every Christmas.

Then there was my subscription to *Beatles Monthly*. It came all the way from England. I thought I was really in the know once those started hitting my mailbox. The excitement of getting those magazines each month was heady. The amazing photos and the up-to-date news stories about them were a big deal. I also paid close attention to the way it was written, even the little changes in the way some words were spelled—it was totally British and I succumbed to every sentence.

Everyone at that time had to try and have the hip British style to go along with this new culture shock taking over every molecule of your being. Well, first and foremost, I had to have the John and Cynthia Lennon brimmed cap. My hat was dark brown leather, and I never went anywhere without it. I was living in New York and the winter weather was accommodating. When you wore your cap, it gave you the cooler-than-cool feeling of walking down the famous Carnaby Street in London with all the Mods and Rockers. Following Mary Quant fashion, I also had the hip-hugger miniskirts and wide belts in a variety of colors. Adding to the minis were the colored and patterned tights, along with the ribbed poor-boy sweaters that were part and parcel of the complete ensemble. I don't know if it was my coming of age or the British fashion influence, but at the time it was all about how you looked that made you feel you were part of the crowd and that ever-present cultural revolution. I examined and mentally recorded the fashion of the people surrounding the Beatles; it was very important to me to be as British as possible.

Following the wardrobe obsession, there was the issue of the hair. The British girls in authentic mod look had straight hair with a slight flip at the bottom and wispy bangs or as they say in Britain "fringe." Here is where my problem began. The straight look was in and my hair was most definitely out. To this day my hair remains naturally curly, and at that time it was quite obvious I had a real mess going on. Sadly, I would never be able to have that special British look. How I dreaded those nasty New York rainy, frizzy days because my look got inevitably worse. I wanted straight hair, but no ironing or product was going to give me what I wanted. My mop of hair did finally stand the test of time and I grew it so long that the pure weight of it pulled it down. The humongous curlers were also a great tool to smooth out my hair, and I learned to live with what I had.

The Yardley cosmetic line from Britain had become the new Revlon of our day. I loved walking to my village shopping area, heading straight to the local drugstore, and checking out all the glamorous products by Yardley; it was like getting on a plane and being transported to London. I was excited each time I entered the store and saw the display. The marketing for Yardley makeup was a multicolored striped pattern of pinks and oranges, blues and purples. I remember well one quirky little gadget, a tiny canister of three compartments that included an itsy-bitsy mirror in the cap, then the concealer. Under the concealer, a little slide popped out and there was black eyeliner, and the next slide down was a light blue eye shadow—a totally mini magic makeup mechanism. That concealer was the key to the perfect look and made your eyes stand out in a sort of ghostly, but hip fashion. The "London Look" Surf Slicker Lipstick was another trick to help you get that pale glow that seemed to be the rage at the time. With my limited means of babysitting money, I always managed to get my hands on some products to get me closer to that British bird look. I would sit in front of my lighted makeup mirror all morning and try to get those Twiggy lashes just right. Yet another challenge, but a must-have, was the white eyeliner just above the black liner on your upper lid (all Yardley brand liners, of course). Famous British models, the likes of Jean Shrimpton, Pattie Boyd, Penelope Tree, and Twiggy, were the natural goddesses of the time, and every young girl wanted a little something of that.

Wanting an education in all things British was also part of the phenomenon. I wanted to know anything and everything surrounding those famous cities in England. The highlights of London and Liverpool all of a sudden became so important. Learning about the city "the boys" came from, where they went to school, where they met, where they played as a group, and who their friends were, were major news items and all important facts that had to be learned and loved. When I read anything about their family, I felt even closer to them. As an avid Beatles fan, I would always dream of planning a trip to the Fab Four's homeland someday. That would be where I could revel in those accents and cute catchphrases that I had never ever heard before.

Postmarked from WARRINGTON-LANCS.A—14 DEC 1965

"Thanks for stamp money we can change US money here… it all helps as 100 don't send any, & some are sick or Blind etc, so I always answer them."
"(3 AM) 'I FEEL FINE' Now"

Chapter 2

MRS. LOUISE HARRISON: THE LETTERS

Back in the day, the art of letter writing was a traditional pastime, but over the recent years the glamour of that way of communicating has become overshadowed and a bit lost. Nowadays handwritten letters are considered rather old-fashioned, calling it "snail mail" as compared to the instant gratification of an email or text message on your iPhone. Agreed, the handwritten letter could take weeks getting shuffled back and forth between recipients, but for me the suspense was part of the fun.

There was a certain charm in putting your letter into the mailbox on the street corner, and after a period of time a response was delivered by the local merry mailman. First, you might glance at the pretty stamps, and then you would notice your name in print on the envelope, giving that intimate feeling that someone had dedicated some of their precious time just to you.

Besides the joy you received from letters of long-time friends, you could always make new ones by finding a distant pen pal. Having a Beatles pen pal was popular in the '60s, and having one from England was very special. Letter writing was our social network of the day; people you never knew before, all of a sudden, were eager to make your acquaintance.

You got pleasure from buying pretty stationery or were even happier when you received it as a gift. Picking out colored sealing wax to match was another ritual. You always took your time when putting pen to paper and scripting a letter showing your nicest cursive handwriting; the idea of any crossed out or misspelled words was a no-no, strictly taboo. Writing letters was commonplace and saying this brings me full circle, and how very natural it was when my friend Jane and I decided to carefully think it all through and put together that first letter to Mrs. Louise Harrison.

Jane, the George lover, and I were friends in middle school and joined at the hip following that fateful February night. For some reason she decided to change her name (among close friends) to Jenny. I think the logic was it seemed like a British name. There was another Beatles friend, Kara, who changed her name to Cory. I don't think I had an alias, but I went along with it calling them by their new names. Mind you, we are talking about thirteen-year-olds doing crazy stuff. Our minds constantly on fire thinking what project related to the Beatles we would try next. Then Jane/Jenny and I came up with the idea to write a letter to George Harrison's mum, Mrs. Louise Harrison. We knew we could never expect an answer if we wrote a letter to John, Paul, George, or Ringo, but what if we tried to get as close to them as we could? Mrs. Louise Harrison would be the perfect candidate as she loved all the fans and the whole Beatlemania movement. I'm not completely sure how we got her address, probably a teen magazine article somewhere, but once we thought it was worth a shot, we sat down to write a letter to George Harrison's mother.

When we wrote to her, we carefully selected sheer, lightweight stationery intended to be sent via airmail. I mean it was going all the way to England; sea mail would never do. Back then you actually had an option, but for us "par avion" was the only way to go. We also enclosed a self-addressed envelope, putting her address in the top left corner and my name and address in the bottom middle. The very first couple of ready return envelopes we even franked with the U.S. stamps, so she'd write back and would not have to worry about paying postage or filling out an envelope for us. I don't know how they got through to us from England, but they did. Then later on we started enclosing coins for her to put British stamps on the envelopes instead (she made a point of regularly thanking us for enclosing the coins for postage). We did anything and everything to make it an easy task for her and ensure a kind response. We hoped anyway. Yes, we were crazy thirteen-year-olds, but one day, these two crazy thirteen-year-olds received a letter from that sainted woman and we screamed for days in utter shock.

Once the impact of her first letter wore off a little, I began to think there was a possibility she really hadn't written this. I mean, logically speaking, how could she answer everyone? I genuinely thought maybe she had some help with all that letter writing. Scenarios always raced through my head that she had had some sort of team gathered with her to answer the fan mail. I was sure she had received hundreds of letters and the whole idea of her answering each and every one was totally insane. I soon learned, though, Mrs. Harrison defied logic; she was a superwoman that went above and beyond for the fans. Over the years as we had kept corresponding, I still had my little doubts, but less and less as time went on. I couldn't pass up the opportunity to keep our friendship going and growing. I always wrote back and she always responded. After a few years, I finally had to admit to myself, *well, yes, this could be the real deal*. Her manner of writing was generally short and sweet. Her form was identical in each letter, and I realized every single note had the exact same script. I also noticed her handwriting had the same straight up-and-down strokes and formation of letters as George's handwriting, which I thought was very cool.

In later years, I had read stories online about Mrs. Harrison by a few of her other corresponding fans and it seemed more and more what I had hoped; she alone did truly write all my letters. Some people even posted a letter or two of hers online, and I could recognize right away the exact same hand-writing. Over time she had become well known for tirelessly answering all the loving fan mails that arrived at their home. From her letters I could see she was the Beatles' number one follower and she understood how we all felt. She promoted the Beatles experience in any way she could, and her support made so many of us happy in the process. Mrs. Harrison's dedication for writing letters to fans reminded me of one of her letters in which she made a point of letting us know she was still at it: "(3 AM) 'I FEEL FINE' Now." She was way too much and way too kind.

Recently, I read a memoir by George's sister, also named Louise, in which she summed up the facts about her sweet and loving mum. It was exactly what I always wanted to know. In her book *My Kid Brother's Band a.k.a. The Beatles!* (Acclaim Press, 2014), she described how her mum was always writing letters and suddenly with the many letters she was receiving showing the love for the boys, she simply wanted to give back. Louise went on to explain how her parents would sit together in the evenings and answer all the fan mail. Her dad would prepare the envelopes and her mum would write a short response to "each person." (After reading how her dad used to address the enve-lopes, I realized he didn't have to do that with our letters. We gave him a little break ☺). Even this late in the game, it is refreshing and reassuring to be so enlightened. I can finally put aside any doubt I had once and for all.

In most cases, Mrs. Harrison's letters were more like little notes. Sometimes she would just write a few lines on a scrap piece of paper or jot down something inside a blank card, but she always made sure to do her utmost to return something to us. How special it was, though, to read her few words and often learn the little details about them directly from her firsthand. She gave us tidbits of Beatles stories that any fan would crave.

Jane/Jenny and I actually composed only a few letters together, and then I went on my own. When we received an answer from Mrs. Harrison for a letter we had written together, we would take turns to keep the letters. She kept a few and I kept a few. I wonder after so many years if Jane still might have any of her lot? After her move from Lynbrook, time just passed and we simply drifted apart. We caught up again many years later after marriage and children, but the connection slipped away once again. Who knows how or why these things happen, but I sincerely miss her. I can only think of her with the fondest of our many Beatlemaniac memories.

Jane and I started writing to Mrs. Harrison in the summer of 1965, and her last letter to me was dated in March of 1969—she died in 1970. She was a dear, sweet soul, and I believe her kindness had everything to do with the George everyone loved.

I honestly cannot remember what we wrote to her in each letter, but reading her replies I get a little clue here and there. It was sincerely all about just staying in touch and getting any information about them that we could, and especially any information from the sweetest of sources, Mrs. H.

It was a happy time when I would come home from school and find one of her letters waiting for me. It became a familiar occurrence after a while;

it was not the craziness surrounding that first letter. My mom would casually say, "You got another letter from Mrs. Harrison." I still loved getting her mail, though, and carefully hung onto each and every word. I believe she did her best to write to everyone in return, so I am sure there are many letters to many Beatles fans still floating around in the world. In my case, I still have my twenty, all in great condition.

During my 2012 Liverpool trip, I found a contact for more information about my letters. Walking along Matthew Street, I entered a shop that was filled to the brim with Beatles memorabilia. It was just chock-full of anything you could think of Fab Four-related, and I left there with the idea that these guys would be a good place to start. After my return home, I emailed the store manager about my notes from Mrs. Harrison and asked if he could shed any light. I asked him if he had other letters from Mrs. Harrison in his memorabilia store. Did he know anything about her correspondence with countless fans? He responded quickly stating that Mrs. Harrison was a prolific writer and mentioned that sometimes she even included Beatles items along with her letters. In the end, though, he didn't even question their validity. It seemed he knew well enough she wrote letters like crazy to everyone, and I was no exception.

The letters traveled to Rome when I relocated there for three years and returned back to the States with me in the late '80s (this is true for all my Beatles stuff, everything stayed with me). At present, this sacred lot of correspondence is still tucked neatly away in my treasure chest jewelry box and where it has been securely cherished since 1969.

Each time I open my closet, though, I am reminded of those letters. There is that treasure chest on the top right shelf peeking back at me with Mrs. Harrison's letters inside. With each glance I can mentally hear her whispers: *I'm still here, come and have a read*. Not often but occasionally over the years, I did pull them out and reread them one by one with fun and wonder.

All the letters are in the same self-addressed envelopes I originally sent inside my letters to her. Her return address changed a couple of times over the years. The early letters were written from 174 Mackets Lane, Woolton, Liverpool, 25 England, and then the family moved. I recall in one of her letters from 1966, she told me to "use my new address, only don't give it out." Poor thing, she was certainly inundated. After that I carefully made sure the return address was corrected: Sevenoaks Pewterspear Lane, Appleton, Cheshire, England.

I am so happy I saved them all as that era was so important to me, and these written messages were a personal reminder of a time that was special.

So along with the letters and photos Mrs. Harrison sent, I managed to hang on to just about everything I acquired in the '60s: all their LPs (mono and stereo), most of their 45s, Beatles cards (black-and-white, color, and *A Hard Day's Night* series), twelve issues of *Beatles Monthly*, a Beatles Photo/Christmas Card from their fan club, Shea Stadium Concert Brochure, and black-and-white glossy photos sold on the day of the show. The letters, though, are my most personal and greatest of my Beatlemania souvenirs.

I'm adding a PS to this chapter to happily say that I finally located my dear Beatles friend, Jane. The three years during the writing of this memoir was three years of thinking of her each time I touched this manuscript. We have since caught up and are enjoying the reminiscing. I did get to ask her if she had saved any of her letters, but unfortunately she did not.

Postmarked from LIVERPOOL F.3.—31 OCT 1967

"Next Sunday 5th I arrive in NY again for a T.V. programme."

Chapter 3

THE BRITISH ARE DEFINITELY COMING

———————

Once I got a chance to watch their first movie *A Hard Day's Night* many, many times, I was soon brought up to speed on their environment and culture. Their next movie *Help!* came quickly after, and I was well on my way to loving and living the British life. The Beatles brought to America something named the "British Invasion" which created my desire to be in touch with the folks and their country across the pond. The new British musical groups, all the British movies released in the States, and British TV shows being broadcast on our telly were just stepping stones and lessons to my further education, which became an important part of my life from there on. At one point, my beloved Mrs. Harrison made a TV appearance for all to see; she was my very own superstar.

In one of her letters, she spoke about the Beatles "film on T.V." which I later realized was the *Magical Mystery Tour.* The film was released in Britain on December 26, 1967 (Boxing Day). There were no rave reviews with regard to this film, so it wasn't readily available in the States owing to the poor ratings, but I loved how she gave me a little inside scoop about it back in October '67. It would be a while before I would get a chance to watch it.

How I loved the few British TV shows we received like *The Avengers.* In prime time, I could sit there for an hour and enjoy listening to those accents. I would fixate on the fashion of Emma Peel in her jumpsuits or minis and boots; Mrs. Peel portrayed the ultimate mod British look. Then there was the proper and dashing John Steed and the stylish array of fancy British cars. I became especially partial to foreign cars from that point on; being swayed in that direction, years later I eventually owned numerous imported cars. The dazzling dialogue surely kept me on my toes and found myself always listening hard to catch every fast-paced quip. I was slowly learning the ways of the British and keenly taking mental notes along the way. This was more than fun.

Along with *The Avengers,* another popular super sleuth-type series I enjoyed was *The Saint* starring Roger Moore. For some reason it was a very late-night broadcast and not always part of my routine. When I could catch it now and again, though, I was pleased to get a little more of that British glamour. Simon

Templar was surely a looker and that alone was good reason to watch the show. Along with *The Saint*, all the Bond movies became even more special now as we began to appreciate that British mood and ambience. How I rushed to see *Alfie* with Michael Caine, to listen and learn. Also, I needed to get a close-up look at Paul McCartney's new girlfriend, Jane Asher. Jane had a small part in the movie, but she was on the big screen. Many a Beatles fan went to see that movie for that purpose only. Then the ultimate in British everyday life came to our theaters, *To Sir, With Love*, which was certainly a classic. This movie resonated with the youth of the time as it was school, but in England—Wow! We all got a taste of what it was like for British teens our age. In sweet cockney dialect, we connected to their emotions and thoughts. (The Beatles were even mentioned in some dialogue in the movie which I thought was fun. The Fab Four were everywhere, and we were often touched by them when we least expected it.)

The television variety program hosted by Ed Sullivan introduced us to a new British group every Sunday at 8:00 p.m.; Ed booked them all and then some. He opened the evening with, "We have a really big *shew* tonight," and when it was over it always seemed a great way to wrap up each weekend. We had lots to talk about with friends at school on Monday morning. Rock and Roll TV shows such as *Shindig* and *Hullabaloo* also gave us more British music than we could handle; it was a frantic time trying to catch every show and every group just to keep up. Musical legends were evolving before our eyes, and we were enjoying a firsthand look. It was an exhilarating musical time that would stay with us forever.

A fun happening with *Hullabaloo* gave my Beatles buddy, Jane, and me a real boost of excitement. One day I wrote a letter to the *Hullabaloo* show for free tickets. The show was being broadcast at the NBC Brooklyn Color Studio and was open to the public with tickets. I ended up getting four seats for the taping of one of their shows. Jane and I made sure we watched *Hullabaloo* the week prior to our event so we could get the full lineup of guests that would be performing on their next show. I remember we were sitting on the floor right in front of the TV in my living room just waiting for the end. Finally, it was announced, "And next week, the Rolling Stones!" OMG, *what did he say*? We hugged each other and screamed with joy; we couldn't believe our luck. We LOVED the Beatles, but to see the Stones live in person was major exciting, too. After all, the Stones were a hot British group and we were thrilled.

We traveled to Brooklyn with Jane's mom and older brother. I remember her brother dressed rather odd that afternoon (to us anyway). He wore a tweed sports jacket, dark turtleneck, and sported a pipe—a rather older and distinguished look for him—and it totally took us by surprise. We entered the theater and the ushers immediately were drawn to him. They must have thought he was someone important, and they escorted him right up to a seat in the front. I have no idea who they thought he was, but I think her brother understood the meaning of the word "perception" and he made them at least wonder. He gave us a smile as he walked past us, and Jane and I looked at each other dumbfounded. The ushers then brought the three of us to seats somewhere in the middle of the audience; but no worries, it was a very tiny studio, so our view was incredible. We were planted in a cozy, intimate setting, and it was so cool to see these rock stars just walking around the studio stage, completely casual and relaxed. They did two exceptional songs, *Get Off Of My Cloud* and *She Said Yeah*. This was 1965, so the Stones performing that day were the originals, that is, with Brian Jones and Bill Wyman. It was classic iconic Stones—wow, wow, and more wow! I recently located that very show on YouTube and relived the experience of their performance once again. It became more than a fun memory; it was another British delight.

The culture and music of England were all coming together rather nicely now. I was given all I wanted to know without having to search. I was getting a nice daily dose and loving every minute of it.

In today's world, we are on British TV overload with the likes of BritBox and many sitcoms or series on the PBS channel. But who's complaining? Those accents are so normal to me now and I no longer struggle through. I just sit back and enjoy. The British are here to stay, lucky me.

Postmarked from LIVERPOOL A—10 AUG 1965

"The Hotels are always kept secret."

Chapter 4

THE CONCERTS AT SHEA STADIUM

So, on August 15, 1965, I attended my first Beatles concert. Phyllis, aka Fifi, and I were friends through our parents and enjoyed the early Beatles excitement whenever we got together. Her dad was able to get four tickets to the concert and told us if we could find a way to get there, we could have them. My parents immediately insisted my brother Joe tag along as he would be our ride and chaperone; that put a damper on any attempt to try and see the Beatles at their hotel that evening even if Mrs. Harrison had spilled the beans. Big brother was watching along with his friend, Nick, who would enjoy that remaining ticket. It was the concert of all concerts, and it was the very first time a musical group played in such an enormous venue.

When we arrived that August evening, we were directed to the "blue" section of seats, which was about three tiers up; then an usher on our level brought us directly to our four reserved "blue" seats. Once we got there all we could notice was a freakin' pole which stood right in front of our seats. How was it possible? A pole! Yes, agreed all the levels directly above us and below us had the same pole in front of them, but I still felt lousy for us. Of course, we peered around it, but what a major disappointment, nonetheless. I cried when I saw where we were with no free and clear view; it just made me feel like I was even further away. The sadness was soon forgotten though, as those tears of pain turned into tears of joy once the Fab Four exited their ride out to the field and charged the stage. The electricity of emotions ran through us all and any control I thought I had soon disappeared. I was part of the roar of the crowd, and the continuous sounds of the pitched screams were the new normal for the night.

Even though we were very far away, it was so thrilling to know it was really THEM. The Beatles were on second base, and we were all the way out and up in left field. At one point, Fifi and I were moving our arms in a frantic wave and at that very same moment, Paul had turned to left field and was facing our side. He then waved to the crowd. Fifi and I looked at each other and hugged. Of course, he must have seen us and was waving back; oh yes, the absurd but yet sweet simplicity of it all.

Throughout the concert, my brother became increasingly nervous and a bit worried. He didn't know what was happening to me as he witnessed his kid sister work herself up into a Beatles hysteria. I do remember at one point, he screamed at me to calm down, and I totally ignored him. The excitement of the evening was by far more than most people could expect to handle; yet, we did, and loved every second.

The ride home from the concert was in deep contrast to the prior frenetic few hours; we were silent. There was absolute calm and quiet among us all, a stillness of exhausted relaxation. What were we thinking? I knew Fifi and I were simply overwhelmed by the fact that we actually saw THEM. This was for certain. My brother and his friend were stunned by this iconic musical moment. They stood among a crowd that was at a level of heightened anxiety never before seen, and I am sure they couldn't comprehend what they had witnessed that evening. No one at that time realized what a historic event we had all experienced, but our silence in the car spoke for us all. When we dropped Fifi off at her house that night, she and I just looked at each other and whimpered, "He really did wave at us." In our innocent bliss, we believed it to be so. What a night; it was a total joy.

Once my brother and I reached home, the first words out of his mouth to our mom as he pointed in my direction were, "Your daughter is crazy!" I paid no attention to his comments, and my mom just smiled and let it go. I think I freaked him out a little, he being my protector and big brother. I mentally agreed anyway; yes, I was crazy. Plainly and simply crazy in love with the Beatles and there was no denying the fact that I was taken over by a force stronger than myself. So, as it turned out, it was a new experience for all to remember and accept. I was under the spell of the Beatles and everyone would have to deal with it.

At home with that evening now just history, I found myself weeping tears of happiness just thinking of the past few hours. How I slept that night I will never know, but I do recall waking the next morning and rushing to read the local newspaper to relive every detail of the concert. On the front page in bold headline was the most spot-on account of the previous night, "56,000 Go Wild." Truer words were never printed and a headline and newspaper clipping for my scrapbook for sure because it meant so much more as I was one of the 56,000 in that crowd that went "wild."

It was truly the experience of a lifetime; it brought so many of my generation to one moment in time. It was a consequence of contagious euphoria that few could ever forget. Besides the thrill of seeing the Beatles, we were all introduced to the stadium concert feel with its massive crowd and enthusiastic energy. We were witnessing and listening to a new form of live music being presented. The stadium venue had been created, and we were the FIRST of attending students in *that* music class.

I had brought my camera with me to Shea and, of course, snapped a whole roll of pictures. Our seats were so far away, and I am sure those photos would have been pure garbage, but at the time I thought I would have a treasure trove of memories. The day after the concert, I walked to our local village shopping area on Atlantic Avenue and brought the film in to the camera store to develop. This shop had been there for years and years and was the go-to place in Lynbrook for photography, music, and electronics. I could not wait until those photos were ready. I kept counting the days the clerk told me it would take and even went in a day early to check if maybe the pictures were there waiting for me. "No, no, no, I told you tomorrow." I thought, "Ok, Ok, Ok. I'll come back tomorrow and get my precious photos of the most beautiful moment of my life."

Next morning, I was up early and had to wait until the store opened to take my mile walk to the village. I ran down Atlantic Avenue and reached the shop. The door was locked, and I couldn't understand why. I put my face up against the glass front door and took a really good look inside. The whole place had been turned upside down, merchandise was thrown all over the store, the shelves were torn down, and the room literally looked like a bomb hit it. I stepped back and then noticed a sign on the window. "Sorry, we are closed. If you left film to be developed, please call this number to get your pictures." What the hell was going on? I was just there the day before, and everything was fine, normal, nice, and neat, with that guy behind the counter and all. Come on, this can't be happening. I jotted down the number and ran home crying all the way. Once I reached the house, I explained the situation to my mom and she promptly called. They were so sorry, and then said they would check the film developing section and try to find my photos. They told us that we should follow up and call back in a couple of days, blah, blah, blah. We called back more than a few times after only to finally learn that the pictures were lost and there was not a thing to do about it. All they could offer me was a free roll of film for my trouble. They had to be kidding! Thinking back of how good or bad those pictures could have possibly turned out didn't matter. Of course, I would not have a close-up of them, it would have been more like teeny tiny Beatles on a baseball field, but the backdrop of the crowd could have easily been exciting to see. I could have relived the concert through those snapshots. It all was such a huge heartbreak and absolute total shock to lose those pictures. Never in my wildest dreams could I expect something like that to happen, a freak incident, sad but true.

My second Beatles concert was also in August, one year later, 1966, and again at the famed Shea Stadium. This time I went with friends—Jane and three other Beatles freaks we had hung around with during the year. We meant business for this concert; we managed to get those sought-after "yellow" seats, ground level, close to the first base. Ground level, what a score! I can still visualize the ticket stub, "Sid Bernstein Presents, The Beatles $5.75." Jane and I counted the days once those tickets were in our hands. Our outfits for the day had to be carefully planned. I can remember my mom making me a beautiful navy blue and white boldly striped double-breasted pantsuit styled with the '60s classic bell-bottoms. We went to the fabric store and carefully selected the McCall's suit pattern, bravely picked that bold stripe heavyweight cotton, large white buttons for the jacket, and a 7" zipper for the pants. Nothing could stop us now. Not sure how it would come out as Mom and I knew we were being a bit loud and showy with those large stripes, but what the heck, this was a *Beatles Concert*, let's do it up right. Mom was a talented seamstress, and I could count on it being a unique one-of-a-kind suit. I guess I just wanted to be noticed in the crowd. Wishful thinking.

The day arrived and we set out to Shea early in the afternoon. Once we got there and found our "yellow" seats, we just wanted to sit and wait for the evening to begin. We had waited anxiously for months; it would be just a few hours more, and to mention we were aquiver with excitement would be a huge under-statement as we were clearly beaming from head to toe, inside and out. We were bubbly one minute, chat-ting up with neighboring Beatlemaniacs, and then super quiet the next. We were feeling nervous for sure and there was an uncertainty all its own. The one thing we did know and told each other was how very grateful we were for those seats. We felt sort of special, and even more giddy thinking of how WE got there. It was a perfect kind of day.

I remember there were police all around trying to control any craziness that was sure to happen. I told one officer I would love to run out on the field and try to get to the stage. He turned to me with my wide-striped suit and calmly stated, "You try that girlie, and you will already have the clothes for the place we will take you. You will be all set." How rude and yet humorous. In all fairness, he was putting me in my place from the get-go—"Watch out, you little Beatlemaniac, I have my eye on you," he said. Well, mission accomplished, I was noticed. It was all part of the hysteria and sheer fun of the moment.

The joyful chaos of the evening did finally begin and actually thinking back now, I could not recall any of the music they played, I could not hear anything they were saying, but all I knew was that I was breathing the same air as they were breathing on that sultry summer night; I was as close to them as I will ever get, and I was *in heaven*.

I couldn't wait to send off my next letter to Mrs. Harrison. I knew it would be easy to share this happy time with her; I could tell her all the news and describe the thrilling night I experienced.

My brother, Joe, also attended this concert, this time with his girlfriend, and managed to get pretty decent "tan" colored seats. He brought along our family Super 8 movie camera to preserve the historic event. I still have the 50-feet-small reel of film (now also transferred to DVD). The very beginning of the reel also had some footage of my friend Jane and me taken prior to the concert. We were all dressed for the concert ready and waiting. We acted silly for the camera and having no sound on this film, we started miming our excitement of the moment—laughing, joking around, and making our fingers come together in the form of a zero signifying there were no days left in the countdown. We were at zero days and this was it, the day we waited for. The remainder of the footage is a bit of the stadium in the late afternoon with just a small amount of the seats occupied and a lonely stage waiting ready and equipped. Then as the early evening was settling in, he photographed the Beatles arrival in the Wells Fargo armored truck. The final few feet were the concert itself. The Beatles were these little people bobbing up and down on the stage, flash bulbs constantly going off, and a sea of

people taking up every seat in the stadium. Here was
the rousing atmosphere that I had lost in my snapshots at the first Beatles concert the year before.
I had it all now and on video!

Those "tan" colored ticket stubs of my brother's
had been tucked away for years unbeknownst to him.
It was not until his daughter was putting together a
scrapbook for him that she came across those ticket
stubs in his shoebox of memories. When she showed
him what she had found, he immediately thought of his
fanatic of a sister and could not wait to surprise me
with them. I researched the stubs on eBay and noticed
they had a little more value than their original
cost, actually a lot more. I immediately gave them
right back to him and said, "These are yours, you
keep them and sell them whenever, if at all." I don't
think he'll sell them any time soon, but I'm glad
those sweet souvenirs are with their rightful owner.

Postmarked from WARRINGTON, LANCS. C—16 OCT 1968

"Glad Janet enjoyed her visit to Harrisonland."

Chapter 5

"HELLO AMERICA"

"Beatles Freak" and "Beatlemaniac" are terms of endearment, a special code for a Beatles lover who was just a little more than a fan. Another one of my friends, Janet, was someone fitting that bill to a T.

It was a perfect *good day sunshine* kind of summer morning along with the usual August heat. Crazy day fun was in the air, and Jane and I decided we would take off early to get in line for tickets to view the premier showing of the movie *Help!* We coaxed Jane's mom into driving us to the movie theater in Rockville Centre, Long Island, very early in the day thinking we would be first in line to secure prime seating.

Once we arrived, we noticed we were not alone in our thoughts; Janet, Marilyn, and Sondra were numbers 1, 2, and 3 in line, but we would be right behind them. Janet, a Paul lover, Marilyn loved George, and Sondra was a Ringo fanatic. Jane and I became instant friends with all three that summer day standing and sometimes sitting in line waiting for the premier. We had a great time all day getting to know one another, sharing Beatles stories and being excited together for what we were about to watch later in the evening. Also, a bond was instantly formed as we all were on the same mental wavelength. If we were crazy enough to be there ten hours before the showing of the movie and they beat us, we knew we had a special connection; they were our kind of girls.

After the premiere, we kept in touch and became close friends sharing our love for "the boys." We would take turns hosting all-night pajama parties just to be together to remember and recite Beatles stories, listen to their music, and analyze their every move. It was always a blast of giggles and fun, dreams, and wishes, in other words—Beatles heaven. We all dressed in our granny-style long nightgowns (which at the time were "in") and munched on all kinds of junk food throughout the night. We newly discovered if you blend a Lipton Onion Soup mix packet into a tub of sour cream, you got something called a "dip." That was a must at every pajama party, chips and dip. So yummy.

These girls were keener in Beatlemania maneuvering and helped to get those special yellow seats with us at Shea in '66. We all remained friends for a while always staying in the enthusiasm of the Fab Four. There would occasionally be that talk of a trip to England we must take. We debated and threw ideas at each other how we would bring about such a trip and then just loved to daydream about all the details. At the time, we were all very serious in our discussions, but for me that journey would not happen for quite a while. Janet, though, was another case. She was a force to be reckoned with, and much more than audaciously determined.

Some years did pass, we started to lose a little of the magic and our constant contact with all the girls did gradually slip away. After a couple of years had gone by, one day, though, I did receive a surprise telephone call from Janet.

"Wow, Janet, it's been so long. How are you?" were my immediate first words as I took a seat on the stool beneath the kitchen wall telephone (the cord would only go so far). The stool was strategically placed there for those long conversations you knew were coming. As we started to chat and catch up, I knew there was something up her sleeve for this impromptu call and I sat waiting for it to hit me. And boy, it surely did.

"Well, I did it, I met Paul," she simply blurted.

"What? What? What?" I screamed in response. Which I think seemed to be a very normal reaction to this wild and crazy news. She then calmly dissected the moments of her incredible story.

She had saved her pennies and finally decided to actually make the journey to England. The very journey that we always discussed in our group talks with our other Beatles freak friends years ago. Here she was now, though, telling me about her solo escapade, and I began to feel really proud of her.

Right off the bat, the thought of her traveling alone made me realize she had a lot of guts. How she got her parents to agree with it, I'll never know. In any case, she did it and finally made her way to London. Once she arrived at London Heathrow Airport (LHR), she knew her main objective was to find out where Paul lived. All that information of their home addresses is well known now, but back then not readily accessible, especially, to us in the States. As I said before, she was a force to be reckoned with and her tenacity paid off as she did find her way to 7 Cavendish Avenue, St. John's Wood, residence of Paul McCartney.

She went on to say that she parked herself outside his gate off and on for days. She also mentioned during those hours of waiting, she made friends with the others there—the regulars. Janet told them her story of her love for Paul and how she just had to finally come on this quest to try and see him. One afternoon during one of her visits, it happened to be the perfect time, and Paul came out through the gate to get into a waiting taxicab. As he appeared, he was immediately swarmed by the onlookers and the regular Beatles people. One of Janet's newly acquired friends got a chance to approach Paul, pointed to Janet, and said frantically, "There's a girl here that came all the way from America to see you." Paul looked over at Janet and walked toward her. He outstretched his hand, grabbed hers, shook them, and simply said, "Hello America." Then poof—off he went into the cab and was gone from her sight. As quickly as it happened was as quickly as it was over. She confessed her utter shock of what had taken place, and I confessed the shock of what I was listening to sitting in my kitchen. What an exciting tale she had for me. I even mentioned the event in a letter to Mrs. Harrison knowing for certain she would appreciate the fun of it all.

Janet did it! She did what we all dreamed. She accomplished the deed. Even after such a long time of not seeing each other, she knew I was the one person that would be ecstatic to hear all about her adventure, and I certainly was. My hat was off to her, she really did it. You go girl, happy thoughts of you, my friend—you made my afternoon.

Postmarked from LIVERPOOL—10 MCH 1967

"The Beatles are not breaking up at all, or ever."

Chapter 6

MOVING ON—BUT NOT REALLY

High school years were still Beatles-filled for me, and Debbie and I grew closer. Many of the early Beatles fans were slowly outgrowing the lads. Everyone was getting a little older and many girls started being more interested in their local boys who were right in front of them. Music had always been the main hot topic, though. The influence of the Beatles created a music revolution, and new solo artists and groups sprung up out of everywhere as a result. We were constantly being introduced to new sounds that we could get excited about and change was happening. Adding to those early years of the British invasion, America's talent began to evolve.

The "hippie" movement was approaching, and life was all about being "free" and "feeling groovy." The late '60s styles of contemporary folk music, hard rock, and popular dance melodies gave us a wide variety of sounds with a dose of fun. We were asked, "Can you dig it?" and we surely did. There was also a sense of maturity if you let yourself be engaged in new music and direction other than the norm. It became apparent it was not just Beatles, Beatles and more Beatles.

Deb and I grew along with the crowd, but we still had that soft spot for the Fab Four. She was my confidant, and we enjoyed each other's company keeping the dream of the Beatles alive. We kept buying their 45s and LPs, discovering and growing with their every new sound. For us, the Beatles were the leaders and the masters of their craft. They were so intense, and their music was incredibly unprecedented. Every single thing they touched was pure magic and will be talked about forever. As they stopped touring and created new innovative sounds from the studio, we were blown away by their genius. Their every new trick in the book gave us something to talk about. It became clear they loved experimenting with totally new ideas such as their interest in Indian music and the sound of the sitar. We gradually learned more of George and his love for Eastern mystical ways. This love became the catalyst in the movement and gave a whole new direction to the Fab Four. The Beatles also began adding full orchestras and classical musicians as background for their songs; they had become so musically sophisticated and we were blown away. Even a simple technique of playing tapes backwards gave everyone another reason to stop and pay attention. Their accomplishments were too many to name and their talents were now obvious to every creature on this planet, Earth.

It was 1969; I was still writing to Mrs. Harrison and still enjoying the fabulous music of the Beatles. It was also the year I would graduate from Lynbrook High School, own my first car, and witness from my living room TV set the live footage of Neil Armstrong setting the first step on the moon. The Beatles would take their iconic steps across Abbey Road for their new album cover, and it would also be the year that the Beatles gave a very special performance on the rooftop of 3 Savile Row, home of Apple Records. Years later that special rooftop performance would mark history as the very last performance of the Beatles as a group. The year 1970 rolled around and the inevitable was presented to us all—the Beatles were breaking up. All good things do come to an end. Even though Mrs. Harrison tried to assure me in her letter of March of 1967: "The Beatles are not breaking up at all, or ever," it seemed now it was really happening and that was all there was to it. The one thing a person could always be sure of was change, and we were getting our share. We were sad about it, but by that time even Debbie and I actually started to speak less and less about the Beatles. It was a time of mixed emotions. The Fab Four were no longer that group of guys having fun. They were fighting and being disagreeable toward each other. That camaraderie they owned had slowly faded away and it affected the fans equally. It seemed to be a sort of turning point, and we just gradually drifted in other directions. We were changing, too. As we entered our very late teens, we were seeking out new and different adventures for fun. We talked more and more about going out, driving around, shopping in the city, and watching a local Long Island group called "The Illusion." Music was always our common denominator. The group called "The Beatles" was now history; a wretched thing to happen to us all, but what to do? Time was pressing on and we just had to go wherever it was taking us.

As I was moving along, the idea of traveling the globe had always interested me and slowly became my goal in life. Getting a job with an airline seemed the easiest way to make this dream a reality. All I could think of at the time was getting on a plane to go somewhere. As a young adult, I was fascinated with Europe in general, and the term "foreign" was not at all foreign to me. I had learned so much over the Beatles years of England and the world from the places they traveled and played at. It all seemed so familiar and yet the adventure of it so new and exciting. Those early teen days of a Beatles/England escapade was always kept alive and tucked away nicely in the back of my mind.

I set my sights on entering the workforce and hoped my wishful airline job would appear. First, though, I decided I'd take the summer off. Mentally planning that I would be working for the rest of my life, I conveniently rationalized I'd better take a little break and enjoy a few carefree months. I hit Point Lookout Beach every single day and enjoyed a Carvel ice cream treat almost every evening. I gained 10 pounds that summer, but I was in a relax mode and I didn't even care an ounce. Immediately after Labor Day, I woke from my *golden slumbers* of the summer and started looking for a job. I pounded the pavement of JFK International Airport filling out applications at any airline that would hand me one. I then decided to sign up with a temp agency and specifically requested any airline job just to get my foot in the door. I was lucky enough to work for Swiss Air and Seaboard for a few weeks here and there. I then realized I needed something steady, so I accepted a permanent position at a boring insurance company close by in Lynbrook. Welcome to Corporate America! It was a good experience, though, and I used this opportunity to keep my secretarial skills strong until that fateful day in February 1970 would come to pass.

My dad owned the local delicatessen in Lynbrook (Frank's Deli) and knew the whole town. He was my personal headhunter of the day. He continually talked to all his customers who worked at different airlines, always reminding them that his daughter was looking for a job, and if they knew of anything, they should please let him know. Lynbrook was rather close to the airport, so an airline job was pretty common among the locals. One evening in February, Bob walked into my dad's deli and stood in the back of the store until all the customers had left. He approached the counter and spoke to my dad, "Hey, Frank, is your daughter still looking for a job?" I was home at the time, and Dad quickly called to tell me of Bob's visit to the store, and that I had a phone interview the next morning with the manager of purchasing for British Overseas Airways Corporation (BOAC). I couldn't believe my ears. Did he say BOAC? What luck, what crazy, crazy, insane luck—luck is described as an experience that is good and happens by chance. Wow, all of the above, for sure. This was luck that was beyond my wildest dreams.

I made the call the next day and set a time for a personal interview. The office was located just outside JFK International Airport in a dingy, old building on Rockaway Boulevard, but no matter, I was in awe. It was a job with an airline, but not just any airline, it was the most amazing British airline in existence. BOAC was the very airline that Lennon and McCartney wrote about in the first line of their *Back in the U.S.S.R.* song. Besides the Lennon/McCartney shout out, the airline had a distinction all its own. It turned out to be a slam dunk interview as they were so desperate for anyone that could type. They just needed to see if I at least knew the home row on the keys of the manual typewriter. After my quick typing test, "You're hired" was all I could hear. What pure joy. The recommendation of Bob surely helped as well. I was in. February 24, 1970, was a day that would change the direction of my life forever.

It was a destined moment, as I recall months after working for BOAC, I did receive a call from another airline wanting an interview resulting from one of my many applications. All I could think was, "Thank God, I didn't get this call before my BOAC interview." I might have taken that job and missed out on my opportunity of a lifetime.

Going to work in that office was like stepping foot in an office somewhere in jolly ole England. Pictures of the Queen were everywhere, God Bless Her. Most of my new coworkers were from England, Scotland, and Wales, so the accent that I had grown to love was alive and doing well in my new surroundings. I found my bliss. I even learned a few new British expressions from the ladies: Lesley would have a "ladder" in her stocking, Betty would wear her brand-new "mac" on those rainy days, John had to drive the "lorry" every afternoon to transport the airplane parts to the terminal, and where was Susan when I was looking for her—Oh, she must be in the "loo." I loved it and I wanted to know more and then some. I was always surprised the way in which they described things as well. Unbeknownst to them, their manner surely caught my attention. I recall on any given seasonable day, Molly would scurry into the office smartly dressed in her beige spring coat, fuchsia hat, matching gloves, and small black purse that hung off her arm at the elbow; with a big smile she would immediately throw her hands up in the air and proclaim in excitement, "What a glorious day!" I don't think I had ever used the word "glorious" in my everyday vocabulary my whole life. She made me stop and stare. If now, by chance, I happen to describe something as "glorious," it is surely with a grin and only in the memory of sweet Molly.

I made friends quickly and enjoyed getting to hear all their life stories. The older ladies had interesting young lives in Britain during the World War II era and some of their war experiences were all too real and a bit scary. They described hearing bombs being dropped and the terror they lived with every day. They came from various cities, so I got my education of towns I had never even heard before. I loved hearing anything about England, so I was always all ears. That connection to England was definitely Beatles-inspired and instilled in me from way back when; it just became a part of my emotional DNA.

These ladies were very well traveled since before I was hired and the talk of their trips to exotic places left me enthralled. My traveling gene was emerging, and they were helping me get ready for the experiences of my lifetime. They enjoyed teaching me the ins and outs of world travel, and I was eager to learn. I immediately took on the attitude of an attentive student.

Being the baby in the office, my day-to-day interests were not really in line with theirs, but regardless, I was happy to be among my newly acquired aunties. They were older—yes, wiser—most definitely! I felt a special closeness to them as I think I had a subliminal feeling of my relationship with Mrs. Harrison. They were sweet, kind, and caring. They all seemed to mirror my thoughts of Mrs. H, and having those lovely British accents made it all so warm and fuzzy.

The group seemed to watch over me like a hawk, as I was their little novelty. They got a kick out of my hippie clothes and tried to educate me on a more conservative office look. At one point, in their fun and endearment, they decided to call me by a new nickname. It would be "Lana Doon"; I suspect sort of sounding like Lorna Doone (the Nabisco treat). We all got on very well, and I loved every single minute of the day. At 4:00 p.m., the kettle was on and "tea and biscuits" was part of the BOAC Purchasing Department ritual right there in Jamaica, Queens. That was another word I had to get used to when I realized a biscuit was just a plain-ole cookie. Their colorful flair was exceptionally British, and for me, it was all *just grand.*

I was especially taken with the casual manner in which many in the office traveled the world. It

was so matter of fact. On any given weekend someone would just decide to go to London or Rome for a
shopping spree. Then we could always count on some
entertainment when our Scottish football fanatic
would take off to Glasgow to catch his favorite team
in an important match and then report the details
of the game on Monday morning. One coworker's mom
lived in Bermuda, and she would routinely catch a
flight after work on Friday and return that Sunday
enjoying a quick visit home. I remember the price
of that JFK/BDA/JFK ticket was a mere $6.00. It was
really hard in the beginning to wrap my head around
it all. I marveled at the antics of this crew, and
absolutely loved the "jet-set" atmosphere.

I made a decent salary, and all I could think of
was in one year I will have my travel benefits and
I would be off and flying, too. England was definitely in the plan someday, but strangely enough it
was not my first choice for a getaway. The list was
long of all the places I wanted to see, and I would
have London and Liverpool (aka Beatleland) in there
somewhere. I would end up staying with BOAC/British
Airways until 1984. It was most definitely a time for
me that would define the term "glory days." I don't
think I would have appreciated my new path or be so
enthusiastic about my BOAC job if not for those crazy
teenage years and my love for the Boys.

Chapter 7

LIVING THE DREAM

———————

Well, my first little getaway was in February 1971, exactly one year from my hire date with BOAC. I really couldn't wait to get started. I knew I would have Europe in my scope, and yes, even Spain, as Mrs. Harrison thought it *was lovely*, but my first planned escape would be a weekend to Los Angeles to visit my cousin, Pat. The following month I was off to Montego Bay, Jamaica, with my coworker and friend, Merle, for the weekend. I was amused when I noticed that they drive on the left in Jamaica, just as they do in England—I loved the connection. I then took a flight with other coworkers on a day trip to Bermuda. It was scheduled just to test the crew on how they could handle so many passengers on the first BOAC 747. This thought of a jumbo jet was overwhelming, and being so utterly British, they were going to get it right if not perfect; they were always a class act.

In April, it was a weeklong holiday with my parents in Rome, Italy. It was another stepping-stone in my life's path. That week in 1971, I would meet Salvatore (Sal), and my future significant other stood before me speaking in Italian. After that first meeting and our whirlwind attraction in a few days, we continued to stay in touch. We wrote letters often, and I made a few trips back to the Eternal City whenever I could. Rome had become very interesting to me on many levels and Sal was most definitely one of the main reasons. My roots are Italian, so their social ways were a bit similar, but also an eye-opener. I immediately noticed this was not the same Italian-American environment I knew. I was a bit taken back when I realized the language was closer to pure Italian than the dialect I always heard. I was dazzled how everyone proudly strolled along the streets in *alta moda* (high fashion). I became enjoyably fascinated by the elaborate three course lunches followed by the *riposo* (rest) every afternoon. The whole city literally shut down and took a three-hour break. Even the pizza was a revelation; there were so many varieties. This was *la vera Italia* (the real Italy) and a cultural awakening. In many aspects, it was as strange to me as England was when I started to delve in. For a while Italy had now become my new passion as England was during those Beatles days, and I enjoyed investigating what it was all about. I began studying proper

Italian and slowly discovered the Southern European way of life with each Rome getaway. I was at the onset of another life, and my years with Sal would take me on a grand detour from what had been familiar. The twist and turn of days gradually leading me to a completely different road; it was exciting, and most definitely all anew.

After that fateful first trip to Rome, I did continue my traveling life, and in the spring of 1972, I finally took that long-awaited journey to London. I decided I must go soon because the Rome trips were taking over all my free time. "If I didn't go now," I thought, "I may never get the chance." Or so I thought. I could see my life was changing even though I wanted to hang on to the sweetness of my past. It was decided that Mom would come along, and we went for a mother-daughter long weekend. As Mom lived my Beatles days with as much excitement as a mother could stand, she was happy to tag along and get a taste of what I was always dreaming of. I didn't try to find the Beatles, nor did I go to the hot spots that they frequented; I simply enjoyed the time being surrounded by the British which was something that I had always loved. My head was still a little in Rome, so I just wanted to experience the best of the Britain of my youth, but I didn't have the Beatlemaniac thing predominant on my mind.

In our black-cab rides, I did notice many of the street names and highlights in London I had become aware of years ago while reading my *Beatles Monthly*; those memories made me smile. Mom and I were there for three days and visited Buckingham Palace at noon for the changing of the guard, strolled along the Mall to Trafalgar Square, and took a side tour to Windsor Castle and Hampton Court. Being well educated on the places to shop from the ladies in the office, we made our way to Oxford Street and enjoyed Selfridges and Marks and Spencer's at Marble Arch. We discovered sausage rolls, meat pies, and authentic Indian food. There was the traditional picture taken in the red telephone booth, and we happened to also snap a shot next to a British Bobby. We drove by Waterloo Station, and Mom was thrilled as it reminded her of her favorite movie, *Waterloo Bridge*. I was finally in the land of the Beatles, but the experience would pale in comparison to the trip I would take to England with Deb in 2012.

Sal and I grew closer and were finally married in 1974. We lived in New York, but visited Rome quite often. Sal also enjoyed this link I had to my beloved airline and the staff travel benefits. We could easily flit off to his hometown at any given time; catching a weekend soccer match or celebrating someone's birthday was something very usual. During those years, we would sometimes travel through London to get to Rome, and often those return flights were a little tricky. Occasionally, our flight from LHR to JFK was full and we would get bumped. That meant we were not going anywhere. We would have to stay overnight and try for two empty seats on the first flight the next day. Those stays were brief and to the point; all we could manage was taking a cab into the city for a nice dinner and then back to the airport hotel. Sal coped with those brief interludes and was getting his share of the beauty that was London. That was the glory of staff and standby travel, but it was all wonderful; London was a great place to get stuck.

Life was good, many ups and downs, but mostly good. Of course, Sal learned of all my eccentricities and this crazy big deal I had about the Beatles. After we first met and he visited me in New York, I remember how surprised he was when he noticed I had every album they ever made and how I knew all their songs word for word. I was aware that the Beatles played a concert in Rome in the '60s, but realized he never had that same interest that I had. Those Beatles experiences that had taken over my younger days were something that never crossed his mind when he was a teen. For him, it was all about playing soccer and watching soccer and more of the same. That was his passion. After a short while, though, my Beatles obsession did get through to him and he appreciated my love and admiration for the group. He knew the Beatles were something more than special to me and even organized a surprise on my birthday one year to see the live performance of "Beatlemania" on Broadway. It was the very first cover band depiction of them ever put together and to large acclaim—an absolutely outstanding show. The nostalgia of the group was starting to take form and as it turned out many presentations like this would follow in its footsteps over the coming years. This Broadway production was a masterpiece, though, and a truly nice Beatles gesture given to me from Sal. The Fab Four were never really his thing, but since it was my thing, he did his best to deal with it. It was a perfect birthday celebration memory and a fun New York City night.

I continued my career with the distinguished airline that was now called British Airways (BA) and took advantage of travel as much as humanly possible.

We had decided that I would go back to work after the birth of my first son, Stefano, and it was a good thing I did. We traveled often with Stefano, taking him many times to Rome, then London, and Brazil. My return to work was not part of our plan, but I realized I only needed a few years to complete my minimum term for vesting rights with BA. I remained with BA until the birth of my second son, Daniel. It turned out to be a very smart move for many reasons, but at that time all I knew was I would be eligible for a small pension totally on the part of BA. It would be a monthly contribution which I would receive for the rest of my life. Being vested was definitely a generous added feature of my BA employment, and as I would find out later on, money was not the only retirement benefit in store for me.

The Beatles were no longer a group, but as individual artists they became icons in their own right. It was in 1980 that *Double Fantasy* was released, and I can remember the excitement of John Lennon's return to the public eye. In the evenings, I would put on his new LP and dance around the living room with Stefano in my arms to the sweet sound of *Starting Over*. With the music blasting, we rocked back and forth to the rhythm; it was again, pure magic. Later that year, John was unmercifully murdered, and the world stood still for a brief moment. I can remember hearing the news during a break-in broadcast on TV that horrific night in December and I was utterly stunned. The chill that ran through me was eerie, and the daze lasted well through the night and into the next few days. He was gone. No, it could not be real, how could it be? It shouldn't be this way. He was young and so full of life and talent. He had much more to give the world and now those times would never happen. I still recall the silence during the Central Park Memorial Service. It was something that shook you to the core and even deeper if you could possibly find a spot. He was gone and everyone was just so sad, so very sad. It was especially heart-breaking when I realized how his mates must have felt. All those memories of the Fab Four suddenly came swooping down on me and left me feeling empty. There had to be uneasiness for the surviving Beatles—Paul, George, and Ringo—and their loss of John was a void that could never be filled. He was too much a part of them and so much more than their best buddy. They had to go on knowing he was gone forever, and this had to be something impossible to accept.

During this period, Debbie and I continued our friendship, but lived in different states. Her mom and dad were still around the corner, so I would catch up with her now and again when she came to visit. When she eventually moved back to Long Island, Sal and I had made our plans to move to Rome, Italy.

Postmarked from WARRINGTON-LANCS. A—9 MAY 1967

"Thanks for the gift which arrived for Paul.
He was up visiting his Dad for 2 days, & I sent
them to him."

Chapter 8

GAP YEARS

———————

The in-between of life happens to us all and my
middle mishmash of years flew by much too fast.
The thought of how the days merged into years and
then the decades just disappeared was unnerving. It
seemed all a blur, but remarkably there was a little
bit of Beatles even in the blur. It had been years
since the Beatles split as a group and even though
they became famous as individual artists, they would
never escape "The Beatles" moniker. The Beatles
would always be those guys, but the word "Beatles"

also took on a life of its own and we were all happy to keep it going and glowing.

Before I relocated to Rome in 1986, Deb handed me a sweet goodbye surprise. Somehow through a friend of friend of a friend, she managed to get her hands on a fabulous photograph of Paul. Not knowing exactly where it came from, it seems the scoop was that it was taken supposedly while he was living in East Hampton, Long Island, one of many summers. The photo was a beautiful close-up of him leaning out of the driver's side car window. His hair a little mussed with slight natural gray streaks running through it.

After many years, I happened to come across a photo of a vintage Mercedes Benz 280 SEL, and realized it was the model car he was driving at the time the photo I had was taken. The little front vent window of the car had a unique design and look to it, and it was exactly the same in both my Paul photo and the vintage Mercedes photo. It was a minor discovery, granted, but I loved figuring out these stupid little details. Another Sherlock moment regarding this picture was when I was browsing the sale bin at Borders and found an awesome coffee-table book, *Paul McCartney Paintings* - $3.97. I bought two, one for me and one for Deb. The book was about Paul's interest in painting and many pages showed his art along with photos taken by Linda McCartney of him during their summers in East Hampton, Long Island; it seems they routinely traveled to the Hamptons throughout the '80s and '90s. The book was an interesting read as well as a discovery of yet another talent. The real discovery for me, though, was when I realized he had the same look in these pictures taken by Linda as the photo Deb had given me; he had his early '40's semblance which time-wise would make it during that mid-1980's period. It seemed more and more likely that the photo could be from one of his summer holidays on Long Island.

It also made me remember my summertime living on Long Island and wondered if Paul was still sporting the hip flowery bathing suit I sent him a while ago. I imagine not, but it sort of brought me back to the time I sent him a pair of colorful "jams" with the help of Mrs. Harrison. She received the package and kindly let me know in one of her letters that she forwarded the gift to Paul's house and that he probably would be sporting them in George's pool. She was sweet to make me feel good about the gift I sent, and her thoughtfulness apparent as she took care of everything; she was a mum to us all.

Debbie, being the best friend that she was, enlarged this fabulous photo of Long Island Summer Paul to poster size and gave me a copy. I thanked her, of course, and rolled it up and stored it a cardboard tube. I was moving to Italy and had to safely transport this along with everything else I ever owned. It stayed rolled up in the tube until the time when I would inevitably mention the Beatles among friends. I would then pull it out, unroll it, and get the usual "Momma Mia," as it was lovely. The Beatles had been major all over the world, and some of my Roman buddies understood the happiness their music brought to everyone. I was excited to learn that one of our friends, Alfredo, actually saw them perform at the Teatro Adriano in Rome in June 1965. I hung onto his every word as he described the concert to me. I was approximately 4,000 miles from New York, but when he talked about his Beatles experience, I felt a real sense of comfort and at home again.

After my return to the States to live, I found the same opportunities to unroll that poster for friends to have a look. This time the reaction was more of a "Wow!" One pal in particular added I should enjoy it and not keep it rolled up in a tube. He suggested that I should just put in a frame on the wall and *let it be.* Why hadn't I thought of that? I promptly bought a poster frame and hung it in the upstairs hallway of my Florida townhouse. I was getting the biggest kick out of Paul hanging out; my Beatles days were coming to life again. After a while, though, my son Daniel, a young teen at the time finally said, "Who is this guy and what is he doing on our wall?" I explained the history of the photo and the "guy." He wasn't impressed. I couldn't really expect him to be as enthusiastic as I was; it just wasn't in him. He nicely just asked me to please take it down. I guess I knew my kids would think it a little silly, and that's why I never displayed it before. So, really no big deal, I took it down from the hallway and hung it on the bottom back wall of my closet. Paul moved from my closet in West Palm Beach and then years later to my closet in Boca Raton. When I moved to Boca, Daniel was older and there was no way on earth that poster was going anywhere but in my closet. I opened the door, I saw it every day, and I enjoyed that brief snippet of Beatlemania.

All alone now in my condo in Boca Raton, I recently decided to put Paul back on the wall. He is now in my guest room where my desktop computer is planted. Paul's photo is there in perfect view as I type. I gaze over to my right and I can see he is leaning out that car window peering around my computer screen and watching my story unfold. What nice company. That photo of Long Island Summer Paul is now finally showing for friends to enjoy including me, especially me. Thank-you, Debbie.

In the early '90s, I was living with my two boys in West Palm Beach, Florida, and searching for a full-time job. On a recommendation from my friend, Liliana, I applied for a job with Mill's Pride, a ready-to-assemble kitchen cabinet company originally from England but under a different name. The company had relocated to the States and set up their factory in Waverly, Ohio. The corporate office headquarters, though, found itself in West Palm Beach, Florida. I applied for an executive secretarial position in Sales. I didn't get that position, but they liked me and thought I might work well with another vice president. They brought me into his office, we shook hands and instantly the bond was formed. Alan was from Hull, East Yorkshire, England, an ex-professional soccer player and one of the nicest men on the face of the earth. Years later, he would always joke about how I was the second choice because I didn't get the original position I had applied for; we both knew it was the best thing that could have happened. So, there I was back in England, if only in spirit; once again that British feel was ricocheting into my being. I was making countless cups of tea, and talking football, cricket, and the Beatles. He actually saw them at the Cavern in Liverpool. We had endless discussions about everything from the County Council to who was playing against Hull F.C. that weekend. Alan is back living in Hull now as he wanted to be near his grandchildren. We have, though, had many opportunities to see each other over the years in the States and in England. What a sweet soul he is and yet another lucky break for me; it was a nice place to work and a wonderful friendship came about. My British connection continues and is doing just fine.

The '80s and '90s were certainly my gap years; a Beatles sabbatical of sorts. I was not totally consumed by the craziness of my youth, but enjoyed a new stage of happenings that brought content-ment and a brand-new life. Priorities do completely change and you go off on another tangent. The beauty is you realize the comfort of family is everything and your life becomes fuller and richer than before. I had more people to love and cherish and enjoy. I also always knew, though, my past loves were rest-ing inside me even if it seemed a bit subdued at that moment.

Y2K arrived and disappeared without catastrophe, but in 2001, I had to come to terms with the death of George, a catastrophe for me all on its own. He was in and out of the limelight for a bit, but sweet George was always ever present, and now this. It had been thirty-seven years that I knew of him. How could I not be so sad? That weekend of his passing, the TV ran nonstop footage of his life, his music videos, his interviews, and I was reminded ever so gently why he was very special. In ten years, 2011, HBO would run a documentary of George Harrison, *Living in the Material World*, which I would devour and watch many times. It was so intimate and revealing, and I would be in a mental lock about this guy all over again. The documentary showed his selfless devotion to Transcendental Meditation (TM). I do recall the hype about TM back in the '60s, but I put it aside and did not think too much about it. After this show, I once again became engrossed in all things George Harrison. I became extremely impassioned with TM and the merits of taking that journey inward. The more I researched about this form of meditation, the more interested I became. I would have loved to discuss this side of George with Mrs. Harrison now. I can only imagine writing those letters and reading her thoughts or concerns. A well-known fact remained though, his one and only ambition was to be "God-conscious." After all these years, George keeps on astounding me and I enjoy all the surprises. *Hare Krishna*!

Yes, these middle years were a little sleepy time when it came to the memories of the Fab Four, which was now only two. The "boys" individually at different times would pop up on many late-night TV shows, and I always tried my best to stay awake to catch one. Getting older was definitely not in my favor. *Wings* had come and gone, but Paul would continue his reign as a musical genius. Ringo had done some acting, but ultimately found his very own niche with his solo albums and then his All-Starr Band.

Life happened and I found myself moving in many different directions. What was certain was that time had marched full steam ahead and that the Fab Four fun was at a nonexistent pace. I was not as crazy excited as I thought I would always be. Yes, as a young teen, I thought I would be absolutely crackers about them forever, but, in reality, I dozed off and took a nap for a while. Little did I know I would encounter an absolute "glorious" awakening.

Postmarked from WARRINGTON-LANCS. A.—16 JLY 1968

"I reckon end of May is lovely in England … I would love to see you when you get over."

Chapter 9

I'M BACK

In June 2006, I turned the ripe old age of fifty-five. In BA vesting terms that meant that I could have taken early retirement if I had chosen to. Of course, my pension would have been peanuts if I took it that early, but somewhere along the line, someone mentioned that as a pensioner I should still be able to get travel benefits. I had to find out for sure. I called the BA office in New York and reached a nice lady who had to look into my specific separation agreement. She calmly said, "I'll be right back, hang on." I, not so calm, just waited for what seemed like an eternity. When she returned to the phone, she officially confirmed I indeed was eligible for flight benefits along with my pension. My good Lord, I had been truly blessed; I was definitely the lucky one. She went on to say she would prepare the paperwork for my pension and send it off along with all the travel benefit details. When the day finally arrived and I received everything, I stood in my dining room after reading her letter and started jumping up and down, hugging the letter, laughing out loud, all by myself. A crazy sight, but joyful all the same.

Ok, I had to settle in and understand what this all meant. It freakin' meant, I was back. Back to the eagerness of getting on a plane (standby, course) and flitting off to who knows where whenever I could get the time off from work. I would travel even for the weekend, which I was very famous for. Even though it was very natural for me, it used to boggle my friend's mind. Diana used to say, "She is the only one I know that goes to Brazil for the weekend!" Flying around and waiting in airport terminals were the best part of the experience. I loved the whole airport vibe and then, of course, the actual journey. I was on my way to new adventures. I had little free time and too many places to see. I'd squeeze any trip in I could and enjoyed every second. It also reminded me that I'd be visiting England on each and every journey. LHR, being the hub for BA, was my gateway to the world. On one of my England stopovers, I could finally get a chance to get to Liverpool and visit a very special place. Maybe I would go around the *end of May* as Mrs. Harrison once suggested. How incredible it would have been if I was now able to visit her. It would have all been so easy. We could have a hug and enjoy a good "cuppa" for sure. The illusion of our meeting was heartwarming.

Yes, I was in my British frame of mind again, gently easing my way back to the Beatles and the fun of my younger days. My BOAC/BA travels were always a thrill similar to my infatuation with the Beatles. Those feelings seemingly intersected throughout my life. I loved the anticipation and fun of a flight as when a song of theirs was about to be released or when I waited to see them on TV, or dare I be reminded of counting the days to a Beatles concert. I simply loved the happy suspense.

My first excursion would be to Manchester, England, with my son Daniel. He adored English football and was a huge fan of Manchester United. With the help of Alan, my ex-boss from Mill's Pride, we managed to arrange a ticket for Daniel to see a Man-U match at Old Trafford. Dan was super excited. I, too, was excited and more than over the moon about this travel benefit coming to life once again. I recall standing at the BA counter in Miami and checking in. I hadn't done this in a long time and all of a sudden I was feeling the anxiety of those standby trips of years ago. I had to reacquaint myself with the routine of staff travel—the hope for available seating, the wait until they close the flight and then the rush of relief once they finally hand you a boarding pass. It was a process, and it was all coming back to me now. Daniel was able to get a seat in their luxurious Club Class, and I went Business Class. I still remember that giddy feeling in the pit of my stomach. As we started up the escalator to the gate, I simply smiled at Dan and could only say, "I'm back."

One trip led to another, and after a few years, BA decided to revamp their travel benefits calculation. I no longer had travel benefits for life. My benefits would only last as long as the years I actually worked. So, my end date was June 1, 2019. With this new arrangement, as they took with one hand, they gave with the other. I now would be allowed to travel with a companion. It no longer had to be just a family member. The best part of these new travel benefits was I would be entitled to one free trip a year in Club Class (confirmed) for me and a travel partner. I continued to have unlimited discounted fares (standby) on BA and various other airlines, but this annual perk on BA was a special added treat. I managed to use these freebies each year selecting different friends and family to tag along, making everyone very happy. There was one trip I was very determined to take, though. I would bring the Beatles of long ago back to life with that special trip. Yes, arrangements would have to be made to make that dreamscape a reality.

Postmarked from WARRINGTON, LANCS. A—3 JAN 1967

"They all have mustaches except Ringo"

Chapter 10

RINGO CONCERT—WESTBURY MUSIC FAIR, LONG ISLAND

———————

In June of 2010, Debbie and I had our first opportunity to see a *Beatle* concert together. Not a Beatles concert, a *Beatle* concert. Debbie had arranged to get two tickets to Westbury Music Fair to watch Ringo (a Beatle) and his All-Starr Band in concert. I made a long weekend trip out of it and flew into New York for the show. I was being a tourist in my native New York and definitely enjoying the excitement.

Being at Westbury and being able to share that gathering with my local peers was special. Looking around waiting for the concert to begin I felt a real sense of home. I was on Long Island once again, hearing that definitive accent among the chatter of the crowd before the show brought me full circle. Living out of state and among Floridians now, the *Lon Giland* accent is something that I notice almost immediately. I was also home with guys and gals of my time, and this was in clear view. We were all "oldies, but certainly goodies," and because of this I knew they were feeling those same Beatles emotions.

It was more than a night of fun with Ringo and his All-Starr Band. It was definitely a night that transported us all on that sentimental journey back a few decades. The show had a great lineup performing with Ringo and the music turned out to be spectacular. The All-Starr Band was made up of some great rock and rollers such as Edgar Winter, Gary Wright, Rick Derringer, Richard Page, Wally Palmar from the Romantics, and Gregg Bissonette, drummer. Westbury is a rather small venue, so we were lucky to get a good view and enjoy the sensational sounds and feel of the '60s. The All-Starr Band brings to life the selective hits of many groups and we found ourselves singing songs we hadn't thought of in years.

Most importantly it was another Beatle moment shared and a night to be etched in our memory. Ringo was turning seventy in a few days and it couldn't have mattered less. He was still the Ringo Starr we always remembered. He looked fabulous for his age, slim and fit, short cropped hair, and light beard with mustache. It was funny to remember in one of Mrs. Harrison's letters, for some reason, she made a point of letting me know that they all had mustaches *except* for Ringo. Well, Mrs. Harrison, not this night in Westbury.

At the concert, we were reminded what an amazing talent he was on the drums. There was another drummer as backup, but Ringo's solo renditions stood out and we clearly understood why he was considered the best drummer that ever was. His sweet voice singing his array of personal hits captured us in many sing-alongs, with *Yellow Submarine* and *With a Little Help from My Friends* topping the list. There he was on stage, our Ringo, an incredible drummer, a singing sensation, and an ageless cutie performing for us that night. It was a phenomenal show.

Ringo is still going strong with his yearly All-Starr Band Tours, and I did get a chance to see him again a few years later at the Hard Rock Café in Hollywood, Florida, with my good friend, Jaymi. It was another great musical event and I recall sitting there smiling and thinking as I did that night in Westbury, Long Island, "I am seeing Ringo. That's him up there—really him."

Postmarked from WARRINGTON-LANCS. A.—27 MCH 1969

"You can ring me WARRINGTON 62012."

Chapter 11

FAB FRIEND ADVENTURE—PART 1—
SEPTEMBER 2012

London

That special trip I had to plan had been decided and Debbie would nickname it the "Fab Friend Adventure," and that it surely was. We would visit London and Liverpool during the fiftieth anniversary of the Beatles in England. We began our excursion on September 9, 2012, and would enjoy five days exploring the places we only fantasized about. I was especially dreaming of finding the direction of George's family home in Liverpool and thinking of Mrs. Harrison and her surroundings. In my many letters to her, I mentioned that I'd love to travel to England and she always replied with encouragement and a very warm welcome. Imagine telling me I could ring her at WARRINGTON 62012! If only I had that opportunity now to give her that call. If only.

The night prior to my flight to Long Island where I would meet Deb, I was settling in at Mom and Dad's house. I had a very early check-in the following day at Palm Beach International, so it was convenient to stay in West Palm Beach with them. I happened to be in another room and heard the sounds of *Back in the U.S.S.R.* being played on their TV. I yelled to my mom, "What's going on in there?" She had no idea, "something Beatles," she shouted back from the TV room, and I hurried in to check it out. That night on the PBS channel was a special called *How the Beatles Rocked the Kremlin*. Wow, what the heck was this? I had never heard of this documentary, but it was the perfect precursor to my trip to Beatleland. Even more special was the connection with my son's very new girlfriend, Maria (also lovingly known as Masha). She was from Kiev, but born in St. Petersburg, Russia. So, watching this show not only gave me a quick cultural education about the Eastern European love for "the boys," but I also learned more about Masha's roots all in one sitting. I couldn't help thinking that it was so funny how these strange little coincidences happen—it was pure serendipity. That show turned out to be a fantastic way to set the tone for the upcoming days.

Our bags were packed, and our Beatles attitude was neatly tucked down in our psyche awaiting the journey. It was not only a journey of over 3,000 miles—we were going to experience an emotional journey as well. This fact was for certain. It was the emotions of our young days, our first loves, and our childhood dreams all coming true. We were going to actually go back in time and relive the sentiments of our Fab Four. Mentally, in the next few days we would become those fun-loving Beatlemaniacs all over again.

Upon our arrival at BA, Terminal 7, JFK, we quickly finalized the staff travel check-in and headed up the escalator to meet my cousin, Ray-Ray (as I called him affectionately). Ray was a BA employee, and being on duty that night we caught up a bit on chitchat. He whizzed us through the lounge and then we heard our names being called for the flight. Debbie was able to get the last available open seat in Club Class and I was in Business Class. I was happy to let Deb ride in British style and enjoy the royal treatment.

We landed in LHR at Terminal 5 and off we went. We grabbed a quick cappuccino at Costa and then took the National Express Heathrow bus into Victoria Coach Station, Central London. Booked at the Grosvenor Hotel near Buckingham Palace, we checked in, dropped our bags in the room, and started our adventure. First thing on the agenda was to figure out how to ride the tube and make our way to Abbey Road, NW8, City of Westminster. This place was truly historic for us. As we left the St. John's Wood tube station, we walked along Grove End Road to where it met with Abbey Road and there it was—the famous Zebra crossing. The area is always jam-packed with tourists trying to get a perfect picture walking across, holding up all the traffic but relentless in their bid to get it right. We watched for a while and then after waiting our turn, ventured out onto the road one at a time and took our necessary pictures of each doing the walk. We then continued to watch and enjoy all the high jinks of everyone else doing the same thing. Groups of people would carefully line up one behind the other doing the exact poses from the Beatles album cover, and the third in line was always shoeless depicting the look of Paul. It was a grand fun event to witness. Through it all there was the absolute chaos of the cars struggling to pass through those few feet of road.

We then went over to the Abbey Road Studio, peered through the wrought iron gate, and just stared a while. The sudden thoughts of the musical legends that walked up those stairs and through that doorway were overwhelming. Even more special, though, was recalling it was the very musical home of "the boys" and some of their greatest work was created inside that building. This moment in time was real. I remembered film footage from a Beatles documentary showing each of them arrive at that front door and being stopped to answer a few questions. Occasionally, they just ran right in or sometimes they would stop and give someone a few minutes of their time. Looking at that door, I visualized those moments from the documentary all over again. This was the place, and now I was here, too.

We spent the rest of the afternoon riding the tube lines all over London catching as much of the city as we could. By the end of the day, we were definitely pros. We easily managed finding the Metro sign, checking the map, minding the gap, and scooting in and out of the underground workings of the city. We felt we were authentic Londoners even if only for a few hours. Then in the evening we were off to the theater to catch the stage show *Wicked the Musical*. With the time change and the activities of the day, that evening we collapsed once we got to the hotel. We were utterly knackered, but knew it was fun-filled exhaustion at its best.

Next day we were up early and out. Just across from our hotel, we discovered a great coffee shop to have an easy breakfast. Sitting by the window, we enjoyed watching the hustle and bustle of the locals while we relaxed, sipping our cappuccino and munching on the most delicious croissants. I especially loved watching the mums entering with their little ones all dressed for school, stopping by for a quick bite. I enjoyed overhearing their conversations and getting a kick out of their accent. That ACCENT! I always loved it. The British had their distinct way with words, and I was in delight listening to the back and forth between mums and kiddies.

After our break, we were off to Victoria Coach Station to catch our city tour through London. It was a great ride driving by all the main attractions on the upper level of a vintage double-decker bus. Immediately after the tour we had lunch, chilled a bit, and walked around to kill some time before our afternoon excursion to Stonehenge. In our stroll, we stumbled upon an adorable little via in the quaint Belgravia section named Elizabeth Street. There on a corner we discovered a small pastry shop called Peggy Porschen that we could immediately see was unique. They advertised on an A-frame sign just outside their door, "ENJOY A GLASS OF PINK CHAMPAGNE WITH YOUR CUPCAKES!" which was something that definitely caught our eye. They happened to be closed at that moment and we dreaded having missed it, but hoped one day to return and give it a try. Directly across the street was another highlight, an upscale pub called The Thomas Cubitt. Packed with locals seated inside and out, it was clamoring with that perfect British feel and sound. We decided we would have dinner at Thomas that evening once we returned into London. We then went to the coach station and caught our Stonehenge tour; a two-and-a-half-hour bus ride to see a pile of rocks. It was a pleasant ride, and we got a chance to relax and enjoy some girlie talk. A little way into the trip, the tour guide caught our attention and pointed out the famous Twickenham Studios. This was the place where much of the Beatles movie making was done: *A Hard Day's Night*, some scenes from *Help!* and their on-screen appearance for the end of the *Yellow Submarine* film. The promotional video clips for *Hey Jude, Revolution* and many others were also done at Twickenham. The quick drive-by turned out to be a nice surprise.

Stonehenge was majestic, and we realized the site was much more than just a pile of rocks. It was breathtaking. Situated in the middle of nowhere, it stood out boldly among the vast green surrounding emptiness. It was an *ahhhh* moment. We arrived at the most opportune time, as the later afternoon sun gave us the perfect light for splendid photos. We posed for special pics with Stonehenge as our backdrop knowing they would be memorable snapshots to add to our travel album of the trip.

On the return, there was a quick detour to Windsor Castle. It was not part of the organized itinerary, but fortunately our guide found a way to fit it in. The Queen was not in Windsor that early evening, but we enjoyed checking out her preferred weekend home.

The castle is set right in the middle of this very idyllic town or this town surrounds this magnificent castle, all in all it came together nicely, and we had fun exploring the area.

Once back into London, we made our way to The Thomas Cubitt for dinner and a taste of the ultimate in British buzzing atmosphere. Entering the restaurant you immediately felt the coziness of an old country house with open fireplaces and oak floors. The menu was elegant gastropub grub and turned out to be our first real good meal since we got there. We each ordered a glass of wine and made sure to clink our glasses in a toast to a lovely day. We were aglow just being among the locals and reveled in our Beatles/Brit feeling. Britain was all about the Beatles and the Beatles represented everything about Britain, and for us the energy was all one and the same.

Liverpool

Up early the following morning, we had our lovely breakfast, checked out of the hotel, and went off in a cab to Euston station. Our cabby was super, and we talked English and Italian football the whole way. When he dropped us off, he gave us one of those famous English catchphrases, "Look after yourself." This was a favorite line my boss, Alan, would always utter in his goodbye to me. I smiled as it brought me back a bit, and I immediately thought of my friend. Brilliant.

At Euston station, we had to find our way around and figure out where to catch our Virgin Train to the very long-awaited jaunt to Liverpool. Once aboard, we each took a window seat and settled in for the two-and-a-half-hour ride. We were finally on our way; this was really happening.

Well into the trip Deb was enjoying her Kindle with a good read, and I just sat there resting my head against the window and watched the scenery whiz by on that drab, rainy day. It was typical English liquid sunshine at its finest, but no matter, the anticipation was building and I was thrilled.

As the train pulled into Lime Street station that giddy feeling in the pit of my stomach was there once again, and we were finally in that faraway city we had thought about all those years long ago. As young teens, Liverpool was always a very distant thought, but as we got older, luckily our world became smaller and closer. We were finally at the hometown of our dear, longtime friends, the Beatles, and we couldn't be happier.

We exited the train and gazed around at the bustling motions of the terminal. There were a few sightseeing kiosks located here and there all promoting "Beatles Tours" and "Things to Do in Liverpool." We grabbed a few brochures and couldn't believe all the Beatles fun that was available to explore. The excitement was mounting. Out the station, we grabbed a cab to our hotel. Not just any hotel, it was an OMG hotel. The famous Hard Days Night Hotel was where we rested our heads for the next two nights. Leaving the cab, we were already in wonderland. We immediately noticed affixed to the front and corners of the building were statues of the four lads, our Greek gods of the '60s, with outstretched arms welcoming us into this Beatles world. It was simply fabulous.

As soon as I stepped through the doors, tears welled up in my eyes. It was a dream-like moment and the emotion of it all was stronger than me; I even surprised myself when I reacted that way. Butterflies flitted in the pit of my stomach, and I felt the happiness of a lifelong fantasy come true. It was a surreal moment. Adding to the mood, *A Hard Day's Night* was softly playing. It almost felt like they were performing in the lobby, and we would see them once we reached the top of the stairs. There were so many touches of memorabilia and vintage photos to notice on every wall of every room, around every corner of the lobby, and up the winding stair-case. Their music was constantly playing on loop, so we were getting a mini concert with every step. Our check-in was quick, and we were off to our room. Even the trip in the glass elevator was a treat as each floor you passed had breathtaking mural images of them on the walls.

We entered our room and immediately noticed a huge John Lennon portrait hanging on the wall over the bed. There was a '60's retro swivel chrome chair over in the corner. The music-themed toiletries were all labeled with some sort of cute catchy phrase, *Hear the Softness Body Milk* or *A Song for Your Beauty Bath Foam*—funky and fun. The doorknob thingy was unique in its Beatles message: *Let It Be* on one side and *I Need You* on the flipside. It took the "Do Not Disturb" and "Please Service My Room" significance to a new level. There was also a little walking map for their guests; it was put together in a booklet form with the title *Here, There and Everywhere*. Even the "Breakfast Please" room service menu was labeled at the top, *Good Morning, Good Morning*. The many creative references to the Fab Four and the movie gave anyone a reason to smile.

We settled in the room a bit, and I remember staring out the window. Staring and thinking on that dismal rainy day, this was Liverpool. We were really in Liverpool, and being there was our connection to them as young lads and to the fun we experienced when we were young, too. We were emotionally brought back to those early Beatles days and the yearning to know everything about this city. It was really all too much to take in. Liverpool had an interesting history, but gained true prominence after the boom of the Beatles.

We left the hotel to find a place to get some food and located a typical pub right across the street called William Gladstone Pub. We learned that you had to do the ordering yourself. You make your way to the bar and order, and then someone will bring it to your small bistro table. No waiter/waitress style restaurant, very casual. Deciding what to eat was so easy; it would be a typical meal of fish and chips and a pint. We were in the land of deep-fried fish and potato fries; if we didn't have it in Liverpool where else could we possibly want it.

After our luscious meal, we crossed back over North John Street, ventured past our hotel and around the corner to find ourselves on Matthew Street. Our feet would be touching the same cobblestones that those early Beatles strolled on many moons ago. It was the home of the famed Cavern Club where they performed on a regular basis and where they were discovered by Brian Epstein in 1961 during a lunch-time performance. It was the place that truly was their claim to fame. We learned this was not the original Club, but a restored version using many of the actual bricks of the original building. It was the closest thing to the historic place we were ever going to experience.

We checked out the Cavern a short while later and snapped lots of pictures; it was part of the Beatles history and we appreciated the glory that this club was famous for. Another pub on Matthew Street "the boys" would frequent called The Grapes was still open for business and looked like such a lively place to grab a pint. After our walk up and down Matthew Street a few times, we caught a taxi to the Mersey/ Albert Dock area. We most definitely took the *Ferry Cross the Mersey* singing the tune in our minds as we cruised along. We then popped into The Beatles Story museum situated along the pier. There at the museum was an exhibit of beautiful candid black-and-white photos of the Beatles we had never seen before. The display was called The Beatles Hidden Gallery. Always something new to learn and we thought we knew everything. Ha! These photos were taken by photographer Paul Berriff when he was sixteen years old and was working as an editorial assistant on the *Yorkshire Evening Post*. They were hidden in his attic for over fifty years and only recently found. There were thirty-eight very informal pics of the Fab Four on tour taken between 1963 and 1964. The pictures showed them in many relaxed shots, smoking ciggies in their dressing room, having some drinks, and rehearsing on stage. It was a fabulous exhibit and an enjoyable rare find for us as well.

Deb and I had discovered that Liverpool was so perfectly quaint and inviting. The city was adorable, so clean, and the architecture was very old-world and ornate. We clearly noticed that one building was more beautiful than the next. Liverpool is steeped in history from the White Star Line head office building with its Titanic references, the Cunard Building, the Royal Liver Building, and Liverpool Town Hall to St. George's Hall and the stunning waterfront setting of the Royal Albert Dock to name a few outstanding locations; Liverpool has much to offer the average tourist. We learned the Beatles had been donating money to the city over the years to help clean it up and make it the perfect attraction and experience. It certainly was a job well done. Besides the beauty of this city, you couldn't help recognize the beauty of the local Liverpudlians; what absolute fun they were. They were always quick to help you whenever you approached them and every single one spoke with a warm and jovial demeanor. You became instant friends. There was also the casual feel of a neighborhood rather than a small city and we enjoyed the local boutiques and shops. There were hardly any of those large department stores that overwhelm you. The souvenir shops close to Matthew Street were very Beatles-inspired so needless to say they had their own unique energy.

After a long afternoon of aimlessly wandering and shopping, we were ready to head back to our hotel for a glass of wine and some nibbles from the kitchen. There we sat in the lounge surrounded by a multitude of photos of all four of them, but the highlight of portraits that adorned the walls were those taken by Astrid Kirchherr. They were magnificent black-and-white photos of "the boys" all taken in those early days in Germany. She definitely caught their innocence and boyish looks, and the display was breathtaking. We sat there in awe of this fine museum gallery setting and enjoyed listening to the nonstop Beatles melodies playing throughout the evening. It was quite a place and a great way to unwind from our hectic day. After a while, we finally succumbed to our exhaustion and, sadly, decided to end the night. We headed for our room, passing even more and more photos of THEM on the way. We settled in for a good night's rest to be up and ready for the most fantastic day that was ahead of us. It was becoming an extraordinary trip. We had only some thought of the drama that was waiting; the real impact of the day would totally catch us off guard.

Liverpool continued…

We woke up early and eager to get going. We started out by proceeding to the room where the traditional English breakfast was being served. Once we entered we immediately noticed on the side wall a gigantic collage of photos. Not until the waitress pointed it out did we realize that the photos were of every single person on the album cover of the *Sgt. Pepper's Lonely Hearts Club Band* LP. Brilliant. Breakfast was yummy and traditional in every sense of British flair. There was an array of customary English breakfast items: eggs, sausages, ham, mushrooms, cooked tomatoes, potato cakes, muffins, toast, jams along with coffee, tea, pastries, and fruits—sheer heaven— clearly, Billy Shears heaven.

After breakfast, we decided to walk to the Jury Inn where our morning tour of the homes of John and Paul was to begin. We found out it was near Albert Dock which was very close to our hotel. The walk was a perfect stretch of lovely Liverpool.

We arrived at the Inn early and while relaxing waiting for our group, I talked to the driver. I had a mission that day. How was I going to get to 174 Mackets Lane? It was one of the homes Mr. and Mrs. Harold Harrison and family (George included) resided at for a few years and the very location that I addressed many of those letters to Mrs. H. back in the '60s. So, I started my quest with our driver. He wasn't very helpful as he mentioned that they don't really depart from the tour and tried to tell me it was far out of town and not easy to get to. Darn it. This guy was of no assistance at all. I would need a better source, for sure.

Our group finally gathered together, and we set out in our minibus through Beatleland. The tour was officially called *Beatles' Childhood Homes Tour* put together by the National Trust. We had made arrange- ments weeks in advance through their website. This National Trust tour was special because it was the only group that was allowed inside the historic childhood residences of John and Paul. We were twelve people in total consisting of four couples, a mom and teenage daughter and us. Beatles songs played throughout the van as we were off to the town of Woolton located just outside Liverpool city. In

Woolton, we would set out to sites on Mendips, the home of Mimi and George Smith and John Lennon. Just before we would reach the first home, we passed through Penny Lane as the song *Penny Lane* started to play in the van. The drive by was so quick and we couldn't even get a photo, but what to do? We didn't know it at that moment, but the best of the legendary Penny Lane was yet to come later on.

We arrived at Mendips, John Lennon's childhood home at 251 Menlove Avenue. We jumped out of the van and stood there in amazement. This was it, the place where John grew up. A gentleman came out of the house to welcome us, and as he unlocked the gate, we realized we were entering the special area that is John. Our guide started off by giving us a brief history of the beginnings of John's life here with Aunt Mimi and Uncle George and then pointed out John's bedroom window on the second floor. He explained that it was the very room where John wrote their early hit *Please Please Me*. We were then directed to view the area beyond the backyard to the left. It was an empty lot where John and his friend, Ivan, used to play Cowboys and Indians and which happened to be called Strawberry Field. The guide then went on to say that back in the day everyone entered Aunt Mimi's house at the rear door, even Paul. This place had Paul's footsteps all over it and eventually George's, too. The guide continued on about the front door saying that no one used the front entrance (only on very special occasions), and the reason being they could save the carpet in the front room and keep it looking new. As we passed by the side yard, we, too, entered at the backdoor and there we were in Aunt Mimi's kitchen. Pictures were allowed to be taken outside in front of the house, but once inside the house, photos were not permitted. As soon as we entered and passed the kitchen, our bags and cameras were taken and locked in a hall closet. The following moments would have to be stamped in our brain by memory only.

As we traveled from room to room, there was a story to be told and the details of the time back then would come to life. Most memorable was entering John's bedroom on the second floor. It was a teeny, tiny space; there was just enough room for a twin bed and small table. The window was at the foot of his bed that faced the front of the house to the street. Many of John's drawings were displayed on the walls of his room. One in particular struck my eye. It was an early, primitive drawing of a *blue meanie*. This drawing was done long before the *Yellow Submarine* movie had ever been thought of. Obviously, his playful creativity was apparent even back then and was there for us to witness and enjoy. A few copies of *Just William* books lay across his twin bed. The series of *Just William* were written by English author Richmal Crompton and the stories detailed the adventures of an unruly schoolboy named William Brown. The guide pointed out that these books were John's favorite reading material when he was just a little boy. Thinking of these tales, maybe the antics of young William encouraged John and brought to life his famous rebellious spirit, one never knows. As John grew up in that house, his taste in music began, and there was a display of record albums from the '50's era scattered around the room. This space had a distinctive feel that brought you back to a time long ago. I still get chills thinking that was where he was dreaming, writing, singing, and just hanging

out with Paul and George. This was the private space
where he would make history in his own little corner
of the world. Mostly, it was hard to fathom that we
were now there in his space as well.

Our guide explained to us how Yoko told them John
would often bring her to this house. They would stay
parked at the front street, and he would tell her
his childhood memories living there. When she was
able, she purchased the house and donated it to the
National Trust to forever preserve the history in
John's memory. We are so glad she did, and so happy
this day to experience every step inside that home.
As we stood at the street before the end of the
tour, the guide also mentioned John's mum, Julia,
was struck by a car and killed just a block away,
pointing down the road. It was a detail I had never
known before, a very sad detail. We took the last of
the photos we were allowed to take outside the house
and then hopped in the van for our next leg of the
tour, and another life experience—Paul's house. Our
excitement was building once again, but I was also
thinking in the back of my mind, "How are we going
to get to 174 Mackets Lane?"

We finally arrived at Forthlin Road, 20 Forthlin
Road to be exact. The street had rows of attached
housing, very nondescript except for the most important fact—Paul McCartney lived there; it was rather
emotional. We rushed out of our van, and there to
greet us was a sweet lady to give us our Paul tour.
She began with a brief storyline before we entered
the house and pointed out there was one important
fact that made Paul's place different from John's
home; 20 Forthlin Road was completely restored.
Mendips had never been touched; it remained as it

was in its original state, inside and out. Our guide explained that when Paul's family moved from their home on Forthlin Road, the new owners gutted it and completely updated the inside. As time passed and the house became part of the National Trust, the interior was gutted once again and the restoration team brought it back to life circa Paul McCartney at the age of seventeen or eighteen.

Paul's brother, Michael, was a photographer and there were many pictures taken of the inside of their home. The restoration team used those photos to replicate each room to the exact look it had back mid-century. After removing the paneling in the living room the new owners had put up, the restorers even found original wallpaper, but just bits and pieces of it. They then were able to locate some new rolls of that exact same paper and when the redo was in process, it was promptly put up on one wall. Each wall was covered with different paper as the McCartney family had limited means and they just purchased remnant rolls. The end product was a room with mismatched walls, but at least they had wallpaper.

The stories our guide unfolded were entertaining and she really gave you a sense of Paul's life with his mum, dad, and brother. She went on to describe Paul's father and what a tremendous influence he was for him. It was well known that Mr. McCartney gave Paul all the support a dad could possibly give when it came to his music. This was a nice thought for us to take along with us. Mainly, it was also a reminder that he had a loving family life, normal and down to earth, just as many of us. That is what connected us even more to these Beatles. They were ordinary folk, yet the fact remains they possessed extraordinary talent.

We went through the house quickly and marveled at the beautiful black-and-white photos taken by Mike that were displayed on the walls, but it did not have the authentic aura as Mendips. An amusing moment, though, was when we were brought out to the backyard and told another story about how Paul would climb up a pipe attached to the back wall of the house to get in through the bathroom window. He would have to sneak into the house on the many occasions his father had locked him out. Once in, he would open the door to let John in. They just wanted any place to be together to write and play music. After our guide told the story, she showed us the black-and-white photo taken by Mike of Paul climbing that very pipe. I walked through the garden in the backyard and pinched a sprig of rosemary off one of the bushes. Was this bush there when Paul lived there? Who knew, but I carried that little fragrant twig in my coat pocket throughout the rest of the trip taking a whiff every now and again.

Once the tour was winding down, I managed to get the friendly guide aside and asked her, "Can you tell me how we can get to Mackets Lane?" She was more helpful than the guy that morning and made me realize it wasn't that far out of the way. I finally resigned myself to the fact that we would simply take a taxi there and that would be it. We decided we would do this after the Casbah Club Tour that afternoon.

Our bags and cameras were taken there as well and locked in the closet. Taking photos wasn't allowed inside. I imagine it makes these tours very special.

It is a must on anyone's list of Things to Do in Liverpool if you are a Beatles fan, and even if you are not. The husbands on our tour confessed they did not want to take this excursion and admitted that their wives made them go. In the end, though, they were so happy they went. They couldn't stop raving how interesting the tour turned out to be and what a great time they had. So goodbye to Paul's house and back to the Jury Inn where we started. We had time for a coffee break, and then we were off to find a cab to catch our next tour of the Casbah Club. The thought of 174 Mackets Lane continued to loom large.

We reached 8 Haymans Green, West Derby area of Liverpool, the location of the famous Casbah Coffee Club—The Holy Grail of the Beatles trail. It was sacred ground as it was the absolute birthplace of the band. This is where it all began.

We had a 2:00 p.m. tour booked from the States through email with the Best family. We arrived about a half hour early, and at first glance, we had a real funny feeling this was not the place. It looked like just a rundown old house, but this was No. 8, it had to be. Still not sure, we started to walk up the street and ran into two local guys and asked their help. They had no idea what we were talking about, "Casbah Club? What was that?" Even though they lived right across the street they were puzzled. One guy had a cell phone and offered to call the contact phone number we had. We got through to the house and explained we had a tour planned for 2:00 p.m. The gentleman on the other end said, "Okay, I'll meet you out front at two." Whew. Well, at least we were at the right place. We thanked the young guys and explained what we were going to experience. They were shocked to learn the Beatles actually played there and what a musical legacy the house across the street turned out to be. It was so funny to us how surprised they were about it all. In reality, though, no one would guess how famous this place was. It seemed to be left somewhat unmanaged, grass was high and the trees hadn't been trimmed in a while. The Casbah Club sign was slightly hidden by all the overgrown branches. No matter, though, this was a fabulous landmark.

It was almost 2:00 p.m. and two taxis showed up. Each cab had one passenger, and they stood waiting with us. Our tour would be just the four of us. One gentleman was from England and one gentleman was from Russia, both Beatles enthusiasts. Rory Best (the brother of Peter Best, first drummer with the Beatles) appeared and welcomed us through the gate. We paid our entry fee of 15 GBP each and the tour began. Down, down, down into the cellar of the house. It had a damp, musty smell, but who cared; we were where the Beatles were born as a group. This was historic.

Rory went on and on, educating us on the history of the Casbah told to him by his mum, Mona. He started with her struggle to buy this Victorian house in 1947 up until how the Beatles ended up playing there in the transformed basement and creating the birth of the Beatles. At that time, they were first known as the Quarrymen, then Silver Beetles, and finally simply the Beatles. It all began on August 29, 1959, which was the opening of the Club. John, Paul, George, and Ken Brown (guitarist with the Quarrymen) went to the club to arrange their first booking, to which Mona agreed, but under a condition

that they help paint the walls and ceilings before
opening night. They agreed and decided they would
paint spiders, dragons, rainbows, and stars. Each
room had their artistic touch, which has remained
there since 1959 in its original state and was
enjoyed by us that very day.

John painted geometric shapes on the ceiling of
the Aztec Room. After finishing his masterpiece he
decided to carve his name into the wall as a way to
sign his artwork. At the time, Mona was upset that
John damaged her wall, but it was never covered up.
We felt lucky to view his handiwork. Also displayed
in that room were framed autobios of each Beatle
scribbled in their own handwriting, describing themselves with little facts like how old they were
and what instrument they played. Rather cute. Paul
painted the multicolored ceiling in the room rightly
called the "Rainbow Room," where they sang in those
very early days of the Casbah. The room, no bigger
than the size of a decent walk-in closet, only
fitting them and two small benches pushed up against
each side wall for the fans to be entertained. It
seems John enjoyed leaving his mark and we noticed
he carved his name once again. He inscribed *JOHN IM
BACK* on the red ceiling in the larger Spider Room
where they also performed. Rory explained John had
done this after their return from Germany and playing at the Casbah Club again.

Cynthia Lennon was always there to watch them play
and being the artist she was, one day she painted a
silhouette of John on a wall which was still beautifully in view. There was evidence of other acts
that also performed at the Club during that period
of time. Photos were displayed of Cilla Black, Rory

Storm and the Hurricanes (with Ringo), the Searchers and Gerry and the Pacemakers to name just a few. There was also an array of 1960's musical equipment, amplifiers, and original chairs. That cellar had so many details and we tried to observe everything. The authenticity of the space was preserved by the Best family, letting it live on as it was, totally untouched. Mona closed the club in 1962 with the Beatles as the last group to perform there.

After we had gone through every inch of that basement with Rory, the tour was coming to a close. Denny, the cabbie, came back to pick up his Russian client and take him to another Beatles site. We started a conversation, and, of course, the inevitable came up. I couldn't resist.

"Do you know how we can get to 174 Mackets Lane?"

"George's house? I'll take you," Denny immediately responded.

Good Lord—that was exactly what I wanted to hear. He mentioned he had to check with his client if it was okay for us to tag along on his tour, but thought everything would be fine. And it was very fine indeed.

It was so much fun riding in his traditional black taxicab as we chatted up getting to know each other. Our first stop would be 174 Mackets Lane. On the way, I told him my story of the letters to Mrs. Harrison and he was genuinely very interested. He was aware of her kindness with the fans and her talent for writing letters to everyone. He talked about how George was the "nice Beatle." Everyone knew everyone from the Liverpool neighborhood, and he learned from many friends of friends that George was really the nicest

one. Of course, he was, and we enjoyed hearing Denny
tell us so. He went on discussing music and mentioned
his favorite star was Bob Dylan. Yes, a Beatles fan,
but he really loved the sound of Dylan. That was okay
with us. He was taking us to 174 Mackets Lane, and he
was wonderful even though he was a Bob Dylan fanatic.
A well-known fact is that George Harrison loved Bob
Dylan too, so there was our little connection.

We arrived at the long-awaited destination, and
it was all really crazy exciting for me. We bolted
out of the cab and suddenly stood stock-still admir-
ing the house. It was just a simple house with a
blue door, but it was THE house. It was the place I
had wanted to see, to know, and to remember. Denny
approached us and eagerly pulled out his iPad to show
us a vintage black-and-white photo of Mr. and Mrs.
Harrison accepting baskets of mail from the postmen
in front of that very door; it was such a treat. He
then said, "Maybe your letter was in there." Yes,
maybe it was. Denny was so sweet to put that thought
in my head. We stayed a while, Deb and I taking
picture after picture of each other in front of the
house, capturing the blue door, making sure our frame
showed the house number, 174. We simply couldn't get
enough. We also couldn't tell if the house was occupied, and certainly did not even think about knocking
on the door. In the past I have seen a few photos of
the inside showing the Harrisons in their everyday
life, so I could visualize it in my mind.

Standing there it was easy to think back to my home
in Lynbrook and briefly reminisce about the times
my mom would casually tell me I received a letter
from Mrs. Harrison. There was her letter in my mind
with that 174 Mackets Lane return address clearly

spelled out in the top left corner of the envelope. Then the sweet recall of the giddy feeling and my stomach flipping and flopping as I opened her letter and devoured each word. Remembering those moments, I was once again teenage Lana in her '60's gear and long hair feeling happy as a lark and thrilled beyond belief. Also, remembering that those years were full of enchantment and carefree moments, with only thoughts of Beatles to consume my time. It doesn't get any better than that.

It would be nice if the National Trust could get their hands on this hot spot and turn it into another landmark. Maybe, someday it will happen. But now there was really nothing on the outside worthwhile to notice for anyone else, but it was a special place for me. The area had a few other Beatles fans here and there looking at George's old home, but I don't think they had the same pen pal memories that I cherished and held dear. Visiting 174 Mackets Lane was by far the most sentimental highlight of the whole trip.

We headed back to the cab and were off to our next stop, St. Peter's Church in Woolton. The hall of the church was the very spot where John and Paul first met, and the rest is history. We weren't allowed to enter the hall, but Denny gave a brief story as we stood out front. There is a plaque on the outside of the building about July 6, 1957, describing the meeting that day and ending with the words of John, "that was the day, the day that I met Paul, that it started moving." The words on that plaque were surely a testament to the Beatles history and a reminder of the place that would be forever revered.

He then took us across the street to the cemetery of the church. He pointed out the very tombstone of the Rigby family and there was *Eleanor* listed right in the middle of all the Rigbys. Being the perfect entertaining tour guide that he was, Denny went on to tell us a story of how Paul and John as teenagers used to hang out in the cemetery and drink. Paul must have noticed this resting place and taken the name from that headstone. We left there with that memory until just recently I heard an interview with Paul and his account of how the name Eleanor Rigby came about. Paul even knew about the grave at St. Peter's Church, but claimed it was pure coincidence. He said that the title song came about from two totally different sources and had nothing to do with this Eleanor at the gravesite. Still, it was an uncanny coincidence.

Then Denny brought us to Penny Lane and the roundabout. There we parked the car and moseyed around the area. We were thrilled to actually be walking our way through those lyrics as the melody unleashed from our subconscious. We reached the famous barber shop they mentioned in the song and entered. The shop was well equipped with early Beatlemania memorabilia and lots of photos of "the boys" getting their hair cut. We sat in the same barber chairs as they did when those mop tops were trimmed and we took our own pictures of each of us. We also made sure to take a picture of the Penny Lane street sign to permanently record our visit. He then drove us to the entrance of Strawberry Field and those famous red gates. It was packed with tourists, but we managed to get a photo in front. The tour ended with a visit to 9 Madryn Street, Ringo's birthplace. He told us that the home at that moment was abandoned, but was going to be historically restored.

This was turning out to be an incredible day. Happily, it was not over yet. Denny dropped us off at our hotel, and we thanked him endlessly. We exchanged email addresses, and he promised he would send us old photos of lads in the very early Liverpool days. He truly was our shining star of the day, a gem, and meeting him was an unexpected stroke of luck.

We finished up the late afternoon exploring some of the city near our hotel and then dinner. Being a bit exhausted from the day's events, we just popped into a local Italian restaurant for some pasta and relaxation. After dinner, we made our way back to Matthew Street and the Cavern Club for a musical evening called *Beatles Tribute*. It was a super show, with Beatles look-alikes performing all their old songs. The club was packed to the brim with people and gave the illusion of what it probably was like when they actually performed there. We stood way in the back in the midst of the crowd facing the stage. We could really feel the emotion of those days long ago. If we closed our eyes, that emotion became part of who we were for those brief moments. It was a short journey back to those times, and the intensity of being in the Cavern. Imagining them on the stage just a few feet away and listening to their sweet sounds were somethings that easily conjured up a grin. It was a perfect ending to a most memorable day. I am still amazed at all we saw and did, and that night we totally crashed once we reached our room. All we could do was lay on the bed in a daze and reminisce about the past fifteen hours.

We were up early next morning; it was our last day in Liverpool. We had our fabulous breakfast at the hotel then off we went to Albert Dock to finish up the souvenir shopping. Afterward, we headed back to Matthew Street for an early lunch at a delightful place. We enjoyed some Liverpool brewed beer and a bowl of traditional scouse (a "gorgeous" beef stew as described by the waitress). Classic.

Sadly, after lunch we had to check out of our hotel and make our way to the station for our trip back to London. We were really not ready to leave and definitely should have planned a longer stay. During our visit we could only think of the warm and friendly feeling we had. In a brief couple of days, we became loyal admirers of this charming city. It was a comfortable and nostalgic feeling of home, we belonged there. We enjoyed every step we took and vowed one day to return to our lovely Liverpool.

We were back in London's Euston station and headed out toward King's Cross station. It was close by so we walked the couple of blocks dragging our luggage through the streets. We took the train from King's Cross to LHR. It was a long and tiresome journey, but definitely more economical than taking a cab. Arriving at Terminal 5, we entered the front door, made a left, went up the elevator, and walked straight into our gorgeous five-star hotel, the Sofitel. Finally, we were ready for a restful night. After our early morning check out, we did the convenient short walk to Terminal 5 and headed to Staff Travel. We were given our seats in Club Class right away and had plenty of time to enjoy what London Heathrow's Duty Free had to offer. The flight was an eight-hour sweet calm as we lounged side by side sharing the luxury moment.

We could not believe that this trip was over and truly did not want the good time to end. We had visited our teenage years once again. Who gets to do that? Being a "bit" older now, both in our early sixties, we were set in our ways of that day-to-day, year-to-year routine of work, home, work, family, work, play, and more work, work, work. This break in our usual everyday actually transported us back to 1964, back to our crazy fantasies of the Beatles and what Liverpool would have been like. We actually lived it. Back then we constantly daydreamed of them and their hometown and now we had stepped inside their shoes. We had strolled up the walkway to the door at 174 Mackets Lane as George did a million times, and we had walked through the houses of John and Paul as they had done every day of their young lives. We had even stood outside the door of the house where sweet baby Ringo was born.

Deb and I had just made a few wonderful lasting memories. We seized the moments and happily experienced the sweetness of our youth. To this day, we continue to reminisce and proclaim it to be the trip of a lifetime.

Postmarked from BENTON, IL 62812—SEP 28 1967

"I am at Louise's in Benton. I brought some letters to ans: to keep the pile down at home."

Chapter 12

2014—50TH ANNIVERSARY OF THE BEATLES AND ED SULLIVAN

———————

It was a special night in February once again, and a special broadcast on CBS would hit our "tellies." The first airing was February 9, 2014. The date would remind us that it was fifty years ago that the Beatles entered our hearts and souls and certainly left us all with lasting impressions to claim and hold tight. The show we were watching that night in 2014 was rightly called *The Night That Changed America: A Grammy Salute to the Beatles*. It would be a very unique anniversary celebration of their first performance on *The Ed Sullivan Show* back in '64.

That February 1964 had been the first time the three of them, John, Paul, and Ringo, were visiting the States. In 1963, George had visited New York and St. Louis and then onto Benton, Illinois, to see his sister, Louise. The Beatles fame had not hit the States when he first came in '63, so George traveled around freely and unnoticed. That freedom would all end once they performed on that Ed Sullivan stage.

The show would highlight the legacy of the band and the impact it had on our world. And for me, an impact indeed! As I watched this TV special and recalled the beginning, middle, and present status of the Beatles, it brought me back to my beginning, my middle, and my present; somehow these four guys were a part of my life and continually pointed me in their direction. I grew along with them and sang along through life with their every song, literally. Their music made me happy, and singing was my way of feeling rather lighthearted and cheery. Their voices and mannerisms stuck with me throughout. Beginning in those very early Beatlemaniac years through my BOAC job and world travels to my acquaintances and lasting friendships, their magic was somehow always sending me on this trajectory back to them. It seemed to forever be about THEM. It is often more than quizzical, though, when I think back of this never-ending link over all these years. I couldn't escape it if I wanted to, and I surely didn't. I loved the lifelong attachment. It definitely makes me wonder, though, "What the heck? What cosmic force was leading me? What hypnosis was I under?" Happily, I answer myself, "It was a Beatles spell," and one that could never be broken, I am sure. If I had loved the Beach Boys or been nuts about Elvis, my life would surely never

ever have been the same. Look at all the fun I would have missed.

That Ed Sullivan reunion night Debbie and I were living in two different states but were spiritually joined together once again, watching, singing, and dancing in our living rooms while we remembered the Fab Four. Throughout the show, we would be texting each other every free chance we got with a "did you see that?" It superbly showcased their lives and music with a finale to end all finales, an outstanding performance by Paul and Ringo. There they were two friends, two Beatles, just playing music together once again. It was a remarkable moment. We were all missing John and George and Paul gently reminded us of them, but really who could forget. Even though they could not be there to share this special night, their spirit was surely a part of the joyful vibrations.

It was also great to share this all with my new daughter-in-law, Maria, as she now had a different understanding of me and what I was about. She watched in Miami while I watched in Boca Raton. As we called each other during the show, I had to admit to her that I was dancing all alone in my living room. She laughed and agreed this show was a lot of fun. With each passing day, we were getting closer and closer and with this evening she learned about me as a teenager. She became aware of the happiness I lived in as a young girl. Little did she know then, but the Beatles would be a part of her children's lives as well. A few years down the road, my grandchildren would know the Beatles and their music and happily sing along with Grandma.

The show was so widely watched and enjoyed that they decided to rerun it three days later. A light bulb in my brain did go off just minutes before this second airing, and I realized I should DVR it this time. I recorded the show and loved watching it over and over again.

After that show it was Beatles, Beatles, and more Beatles just about everywhere. There were lots of fun clips of them on the news reminding us all of fifty years ago today. There would be plenty to talk about with all your old buddies after that night. They made everyone so happy and in a great mood. The Beatles were never really forgotten over the years, and their popularity was apparent once again as the generation that adored them was older and that sentimental yearning of the past was not slowly settling in—it was definitely here. The "good old days" actually turned out to be a nice place to visit. We were welcoming those compelling emotions of the sixties and realized that gentle touch to our hearts had been captured yet again.

This get-together of Beatlemania brought to mind many memories for me and sent me once again on a path full of fun and wonder. They were always an inspirational force in my youth, egging me on in new and different directions. Even now I realize the new road I am traveling and the place they have taken me; I am writing a memoir, and for me, this is more than shock and surprise.

Postmarked from WARRINGTON-LANCS. A—14 MCH 1966

"I know George composed a song on March 10th my birthday. No name yet!"

Postmarked from WARRINGTON, LANCS. A—12 MCH 1968
"I had a letter for my Birthday 10th. He is very well & happy."

Chapter 13

FAB FRIEND ADVENTURE—PART 2—MARCH 2015

So, here we go again. Here is where Deb and I decide to take off on another adventure together to celebrate our friendship. We would plan this trip in March. A month that is not very exciting or pleasant. New York's hard winter is winding down, but not quite over yet. It's not clear how it will be, freezing cold or the onset of spring. My grandmother's favorite phrase was *Marzo è pazzo* (March is crazy) when describing the month's weather. Even though March was a bit of an unusual month, for me there was something very sweet and memorable about it as well. I recall from a couple of Mrs. Harrison's letters that her birthday was on March 10. In an earlier letter from 1966, she told Jane and me that George had written a song on her birthday. I would still love to know the name of the song he wrote and if it was ever recorded. Then in 1968, she let me know he had written her a letter on her special day. A thoughtful lad and loving son—that was George.

Our late-winter getaway would include a little London Beatles to the mix, and to broaden our horizons, a day trip to Brussels. We traveled on my annual BA free trip for that year. It was a full flight, and we were not able to get that famous Club Class. They gave us the best seats available in their lovely Coach section. No complaints here, it was all good.

Once we arrived in our precious England, we set out to our hotel and settled in. Decisions were made and we were off to Leicester Square to buy tickets for the London production of *Beautiful* for that evening. We had heard rave reviews from New York and knew this was the show to see.

We then walked around the city area and were able to visit places that Debbie only saw the first time from the double-decker bus tour. We were up close and personal to the zone around Buckingham Palace, Big Ben, and Westminster Abbey and thoroughly enjoyed checking out all the souvenir shops accompanying these hot spots showcasing Beatles memorabilia. We were deluged with Fab Four goodies during our walking tour, and we were thrilled. Eventually, we found ourselves on Elizabeth Street and had arrived to our favorite area of the city, Belgravia. It's a part of London that is so pristine and quaint. We would discover later that it was the area where Brian Epstein had a flat and was visited by "the boys" on numerous occasions.

We popped in at Peggy Porschen to take a peek at the sweets and treats as we remembered this pretty little place the last time we were in London. It had been closed then and we knew on this trip we would have to give it a try, but not now—we were hungry for a meal! We looked around a moment and left to cross-over the street and enjoy lunch at our favorite pub, The Thomas Cubitt. We decided we had to try their signature fish and chips this time and, of course, a pint. I mean, where else would we want to be? For us it was so genuinely British, and we felt so comfort-able among the crowd of unknown friends. The essence of the pub was top-notch and the sounds of glasses clinking and cheery laughter were ever present.

After our lovely British feel and yummy meal, we made our way to Portobello Road in Notting Hill for sightseeing. It was definitely classic old London. We passed by the upstairs flat of George Orwell at 22 Portobello Road and took some pictures of his home with the English Heritage blue plaque adorning the outside, "GEORGE ORWELL 1903-1950 NOVELIST & POLITICAL ESSAYIST LIVED HERE." We were impressed. Shortly after our fill of exploring the street and wandering through the vintage shops, Debbie and I cabbed it back into central London near the area of the Aldwych Theatre where we would see the musical *Beautiful* that evening.

Beautiful was to say the least, beautiful. It was a wonderful rendition of Carol King's songs and portrayal of her life story. We never knew all the popular music she wrote for other performers until that evening. Those tunes brought us back to our reminiscent Beatles sounds of the '60s and that combination was a grand detour down that memory lane.

The next day we were off to St. Pancras railway station for our day trip to Brussels. Adventure awaited and we were ready. It turned out to be an enjoyable few hours' visit, and we entertained ourselves with some specialties of Belgium—chocolate, waffles, fries, beer—and tried to find that statue of the little boy peeing in the fountain, the famous Manneken Pis. We also took in a bit of culture at the René Magritte Museum and were amazed at his works. Of course, there is always a Beatles connection somehow, somewhere in our path and this was no exception. Magritte was the surrealist artist who created the many famous Apple paintings which happened to be the inspiration for the Apple Records logo. How on earth could we miss this iconic museum? When planning this visit, I recalled reading years back about Paul's love for Magritte in the *Paul McCartney Paintings* book I purchased in the sale bin at Borders. It was written that Paul regarded Magritte as the premier surrealist painter, and his influence on Paul's own painting is considerable. It was so exciting to tie it all into our little side trip to Brussels.

We returned to London late that same evening and headed straight for our hotel as we were totally worn out. Next day, we would experience London on our private Beatles Tour and hit all the hot spots the Boys traveled while they were living there. In the morning after surrendering to a fabulous English breakfast, our guide, Mark, picked us up at the hotel and off we were.

"On a scale of 1 to 10, how would you rate your knowledge of the group?" was Mark's opening question to us as he pulled away from the curb in our vintage black taxicab.

"Eleven," we calmly responded in unison.

Okay, now he fully understood and knew we meant business. He was twenty-six years young, so his real knowledge of the Beatles was somewhat limited, but he did have a few pieces of information that caught us by surprise. I am sure, though, he realized he could not hand us any nonsense story about them because we probably knew all the facts before he was born.

We started our tour with Brian Epstein's house in Belgravia. Interestingly enough, he had photos of "the boys" in front of many of the locations he would take us to. Debbie and I replicated the poses they had in their photos and took our own photos in the same stance.

Mark then took us to an apartment located at 34 Montagu Square. This flat was originally leased by Ringo for a brief period of time. After Ringo had moved out, he sublet the apartment to John and Yoko, and they took up residence there for a few months. This was the famous location where John and Yoko would take the photo that would become the cover for their *Two Virgins* album and more famously known for the location they were later busted for possession of marijuana. It now proudly adorns the English Heritage Blue Plaque honoring John Lennon, musician and songwriter, as he lived there in 1968 (and just happened to get arrested there as well!).

We went on to 57 Wimpole Street, the home of Jane Asher's parents and where Paul and Jane lived together for quite a while. Paul and John wrote *I Want to Hold Your Hand* in the front basement room of the house. We learned that Paul wrote the tune for *Yesterday* on the piano in his attic bedroom. He also wrote many other songs in the Asher home the likes of *Here, There and Everywhere, And I Love Her, Every Little Thing* and *I'm Looking Through You* which, supposedly, were all about Jane. Imagine it all, really. Imagine Paul living in your house, writing songs and creating history right under your roof. Simply put, too much! Living there, though, he seemed to enjoy a sweet family life.

We then visited the London Palladium with its spectacular billboard out in front that just screamed in our minds, "The Beatles performed here!" I had often seen photos of the Boys performing on the Palladium stage, but this close-up view of the outside of the theater was impressive.

Next stop on the tour was 3 Savile Row, the headquarters of Apple Corps. Looking up we could only imagine their famous last performance on the rooftop of that building. We all have enjoyed seeing the video of them of up there singing on that cool windy day. The way they looked, Paul with full beard and wearing a stylish suit, George and John in their furry jackets, and Ringo in his red slicker mac, all sporting longish hair and moving and grooving along to *Get Back*. It was a very special music video for sure. But, here and now we were downstairs just looking up and simply feeling the sway of the song in our soul. It was magic.

Mark also took us to the home on Cavendish Avenue that Paul had shared with Jane Asher for a brief time. This was also the place where my friend, Janet, shared a handshake with Paul back in the late '60s. It was wonderful to be there and remember my friend's story once again.

We ultimately ended up at Abbey Road. At Abbey Road we did the famous walk across again, but this time together and Mark took the photo for us. It was also a sort of reunion of sentiments for Debbie and I to be there doing the walk and talking the talk. There were the usual crazy crowds and camaraderie of Beatles fans all trying to get that perfect picture. The street has its own emotional attachment to the world. This is the place. This is the famous place of the Beatles crossing a street. Just a street where ordinary people have walked across a gazillion times before, but now it was a bit special and no cross-walk will ever be as famous as this one. This zebra zigzag painting on this tiny Abbey Road in St. John's Wood, London, would become iconic and everlasting.

We lovingly remembered our last visit and the glory of that moment never waned. We wrote our names on the wall outside the Abbey Road Studio—*Debbie, Lana and Mark, March 15, 2015.*We were in our Beatles mode and feeling fine.

Ending our tour, Mark dropped us off at the world-renowned Harrods, where we spent a lovely few hours shopping and enjoying a lunch of bangers and mash in one of their many outstanding restaurants. This store was truly an event with a variety of the super elegant to the absolute fun. It was a real happening place and so much more than just a department store; it depicted world-class British style.

We finalized the afternoon enjoying a stop at Peggy Porschen; it happened to be Mum's Day in Britain. The three tables they had inside were occupied as it was such a mum-and-daughter kind of place to savor the day. We knew for us it was a must to get in as we were leaving London in a few hours. We were going to do anything to get that cupcake. You surely get the feeling that you've entered a fairy tale once you open the front door. It's such a girlie corner of the world, everything decorated in pretty pinks and pastels and lovely crystal chandeliers. We marveled at all the unique and colorful treats, and finally enjoyed our cupcake and spot of tea. It was utterly sublime.

It was time to go. *No, please we don't want to,* but we had to start that homeward journey. Our first leg of the trip would be taking the bus at Victoria Coach Station to LHR, Terminal 3, and then the underground to Terminal 5. We checked in at the Sofitel conveniently attached to the terminal and enjoyed one night's respite before our flight next day. It was our favorite stop between stops. Up very early next morning, we walked over to Staff Travel and did our staff check-in. We were regulars now, knowing exactly what to do and exactly where to go. It was Club Class home for the both of us once again, and as always, our many thanks to BA. They just keep on giving and giving, and the feeling is sensational.

Postmarked from WARRINGTON-LANCS. A—24 MAY 1966

"Pattie did a days modelling recently, while George was busy on Recordings."
"I was happy for him & Pattie. He told me Xmas."

Chapter 14

MEET AND GREET—PATTIE BOYD

———————

It was a non-eventful Sunday, and I was casually internet surfing. One site led me to another and for some reason I came across a website highlighting Pattie Boyd and her photography. She and Henry Diltz, rock photographer, were doing a tour showcasing photos of their work. The show was called *Behind the Lens*. As I kept reading, I noticed one of the tour dates would take them to the Kravis Center in West Palm Beach, Florida. I mentioned the show to Debbie the next time we spoke, and she calmly said, "Why don't you go?" Yes, why don't I go? Of course,

I would have to go alone, but so what? Then I got a little excited, went online, bought my ticket, and waited for the day: April 13, 2016.

The day came, and I decided I would just drive over to the Kravis Center right after work. I arrived early and after a while of walking around, I finally headed up the stairs to the room where the show would be. Then out of nowhere the elevator doors opened and there walking toward me was the famous Pattie Boyd. I was totally awestruck. All I could do was smile and she smiled back. She walked past me with Henry Diltz and her handler or manager or agent. I didn't know who that other guy was, and I didn't care. After they went into a room, I immediately texted Deb to let her know what had just taken place. She wrote back, "Just think, the woman who married George Harrison and Eric Clapton just smiled at you."

Ten minutes or so later, Henry came out and chatted with a few people that had been hanging around and then the handler/manager/agent came out. He talked with a Kravis usher discussing the meet and greet about to happen and how it should be handled. Meet and greet? I was enjoying this. He then waved the few people that were around to come on in and looked my way.

"Oh no, I didn't pay for this," I quickly said as he caught me by surprise.

"Oh, come in, don't worry about it," was his sweet response, knowing it really didn't matter.

This handler/manager/agent was now my new friend; and I could have hugged him right there and then. I got to the door and there was Pattie waving at me to come in. What the hell was I doing there? Was this really happening? I walked into the small room with the other guests and stood there a little amazed. Henry came around and socialized with everyone; we spoke briefly and I took some pictures with him. I then managed to get near Pattie and was listening to a conversation she was having with another guest. This person asked her if she ever did any acting. She mentioned she only did one movie and had said only one word.

"Prisoners?" I chimed in over her shoulder trying to imitate her British accent. She immediately turned to me and smiled.

Yes, I had known the one word she said in the movie *A Hard Day's Night*. The gentleman she was talking to didn't understand, but as I knew the whole dialogue from the film, I couldn't help myself. Now I was part of their conversation and we got a chance to exchange a few words. We talked about her interest in meditation. I had been intrigued by TM for a while now and knew it was very much a part of her life years ago. She had said she wished she could meditate more and would love to get back to it. I then asked her to take some pictures together. She was very kind and obliged. Up close and personal, I could see she was still a beauty. She wore her hair up in a high ponytail/bun and still had that lovely wispy fringe. Taller than me, we stood side by side and she gently put her arm around my shoulder. I was more than stunned and couldn't believe I was standing next to her posing for a quick snapshot.

It was getting near to the close of the meet and greet, and the show was going to begin shortly. We all left the room and stood outside in the atrium waiting until the auditorium doors opened. Standing there it hit me, why didn't I ask her about Mrs. Louise Harrison? She was her mother-in-law and my pen pal for almost four years, for crying out loud! Why didn't I bring her up! I think it would have been more than fun to discuss that sweet lady we both had in common. The only way I can rationalize to myself this incredible mishap was that I was in total shock. I thought I was just going to a show; I'd be in the audience a fair distance away and that would be that. I NEVER dreamed I would be standing two inches away from her having a one-on-one conversation. Sadly, a true missed opportunity.

The doors finally opened and I found my seat. I was up close, but over to the left side of the stage. While we were waiting for the show to begin, Beatles music was playing throughout the theater. They were all familiar songs that everyone knew, but not the exact soundtrack. Later, at the start of the show, Henry announced the music we were listening to was Pattie's personal mix of tapes she had while living with George. Back in the day, the other Beatles would come over their house to practice and jam. The reel-to-reel recorder was always ready and waiting to capture their creative genius. This music we were hearing that evening was the product of those many sessions. How incredibly lucky I was to be there and experience these very rare renditions. Sadly, each Beatles melody rolled into another and I couldn't name them now if I tried, but I recall those calming effects warming us all up for what was to become a wonderful show.

Pattie walked out onto the stage and sat down on a stool over to the right side. I quickly noticed she let her hair down from her ponytail and gave us all the sudden look of our Pattie Boyd of the '60s. She was truly lovely, and her presence simply reminded us all she was one of the original "mod" supermodels. As we sat attentively, we were also aware that she was very much a part of the Beatles nostalgia.

One by one she vividly described each photo being displayed on a large screen center stage with a where and when explanation of that time in her life. Many pics were with George, but she had more shots during her time spent with Eric Clapton. Her photos were definitely evidence of her creative talent, and I was especially enamored with one of George and her together. It was taken in 1968 and called "Rose Garden." She described it as tripod set to capture them with the first bloom of the roses in their garden. I had never seen it before and felt it was sort of special and quizzical at the same time. George is shirtless, standing behind her and looking rather serious but calm. He was staring away from the camera over her left shoulder. Pattie is looking straight into the camera. No smiles, just the two of them standing in their garden, but seemingly very peaceful. George, though, looked like he was pondering something, and this photo is open to a lot of interpretation.

Pattie was definitely more than a talented photographer. I left the theater that evening very "Pattie Boyd excited" and also inspired by the art of both Pattie and Henry. In my past, I had studied black-and-white photography, taking a few printing and developing classes along the way. There was a time that I wouldn't think of going anyplace without my Nikon F2 hanging off my neck; it was all about being ready to snap that perfect shot. So, I understood their passion and this show was a twofer for me, art and Beatles.

Pattie's personal collection of George's pictures once again gave me that reminiscent feeling with a dose of sentimentality. In my lifetime, the Beatles memories were always tucked nicely and neatly away, but always ready to make any resurgence when the timing was right. Happily, many times something would just click and I would be off and running. This night with Pattie Boyd was an absolute thrill, and I had that Beatles glow once again.

Postmarked from WARRINGTON-LANCS. A—25 MAY 1967

Black and white photo postcard of The Beatles with "Love to Lana. Louise Harrison" written on the back.

Chapter 15

BEATLES STUFF

Along with the personal vintage Beatles memorabilia I acquired in the sixties, the memorabilia given to me from Mrs. Harrison is by far my greatest of all treasures, and I love each and every single piece. Over the years, I have gradually accumulated Beatles stuff unwittingly by accident or given to me as gifts. For all my family and friends who know and (I would like to think) love me, it's a given when it comes to merchandise related to the Beatles. It is actually a force stronger than them to see something with a Beatles label and not think of me. Many friends along the way have donated some of their Beatles goodies to me. They have books or CDs that really don't interest them anymore and think "What to do?" and they give it to me. They think it is going to someone who will cherish, appreciate, and, most of all, take care of them. This is true. Funny enough, even though I was that aging Beatlemaniac, my fanaticism made some of them think of their happy youthful times as well, and I believe they secretly lived vicariously through my nutty behavior.

I remember back in the early '90s with the revelation of a music CD and how popular it was becoming the sound format of the future. New music was now being sold on this little silver disc, and, eventually, every tune that was ever on an LP was being transferred to this little round shiny thing. Then over time, the transformation of all Beatles music to CDs evolved. Oh, my Lord, I had to have these, too. So, little by little I started my collection, leaving me now with many duplicates of their music catalog, on vinyl and CD. I recall standing in line at Best Buy to purchase the first release of *The Beatles Anthology* CD set. This stunt brought me back a little, and standing there, I remember briefly thinking to myself, "What the hell are you doing standing in line for a Beatles CD? Are you kidding?" And it surely brought to mind those many other Beatles lines. There was always a line to get a ticket to a Beatles movie and then there was another line to get into the theater. Watching both movies numerous times kept me in a line mode most of the time. Then, of course, there was the moment of a newly released album or 45. You could bet there would be a line. So, at the beginning of the CD, having their music presented to me all over again was a comfort—sweet and sound. What was another line? I was a loving fan through and through. I stood there and bought *The Beatles Anthology* set.

I do try and keep the Beatles-like items displayed in my home at a minimum, but sometimes I just can't help it. If you open my kitchen cupboard you will immediately notice four 10 oz. glasses with pictures of Beatles plastered on them. The glasses were a gift from my daughter-in-law, Maria, when we first met. They are my everyday glasses and used by me every day. And there's my Yellow Submarine ceramic bank from my other daughter-in-law, Claudia. She and my grandson, Alessandro, absolutely had to buy it for me when they saw it. *Yellow Submarine* was the one song I decided to teach Alessandro if he was to know anything about the Fab Four.

The numerous coffee-table books about them are within a short reach and I enjoy just picking one up and finding a spot to read and review. It's a time that adds something to my quiet, serene moments.

I do have a rather special piece of Lennon art; I am happy to say it is prominently framed and displayed. I invested in a numbered lithograph of John Lennon's *Steel and Glass* with Yoko's original signature. I went to an art exhibition in West Palm Beach of John Lennon's work and decided I had to have something of substance and worth to appreciate. *Steel and Glass* was his typical scribbled graphic-style drawing of which I knew and loved. Sweet memories of the artwork from his books *In His Own Write* and *A Spaniard in the Works* became reminiscent. I usually second-guess myself when it comes to purchases like this, but once the decision was made, I was happy I jumped in and did it.

Speaking of art, one year for my birthday, Maria presented me with a special oversized card she crafted using Andy Warhol Pop Art computer graphic images of the Beatles and my family. She aligned the four lads side by side and then added photos of herself, Daniel, Claudia, Alessandro, and Stefano. The row of photos is positioned in a way that sort of gives the resemblance of a piano keyboard. She headed it with the opening lyrics to the Beatles' *Birthday* song, put the date, June 1, 2013, and lastly added at the bottom in big letters "HAPPY BIRTHDAY, MOM!" all in Beatles font. It is simply an ingenious creation and beautifully framed on the wall in my bedroom. The Beatles alongside my loved ones, how great is that?? It became a beloved family portrait. At a very early age, my grandson, Alessandro, would love to go over to the card and point to each individual character, and proudly call each out by name, "John, Paul, George, Ringo, Aunt Maria, Uncle Dan, Mommy, Alessandro, and Papai!" Papai was in a loud resounding end to his ritual sing song. What fond memories I have with these Beatles. They are part of my family memories, and I will cherish what is deep inside forever.

There are many other special gifts I adore such as the DVD of *Good Ol' Freda* from my brother. This movie was a unique find by him and a delight for me. After watching this video, I quickly referred to my stash of *Beatles Monthly* magazines from the '60s to find Freda Kelly as the author of the Official Beatles Fan Club Newsletter in each issue (I loved connecting these Beatle dots, what fun). My brother also purchased for me a DVD of the Beatles concert in Washington, D.C., February 11, 1964, a real throwback to those early live performance days. DVDs such as *A Hard Day's Night*, *Help!*, *Yellow Submarine*, and *The Beatles Anthology* are a staple in any Beatles collection and mine was no different. I really didn't need to buy *A Hard Day's Night*, as it is often broadcast on TCM, and I catch it every now and again. This, I might add, makes me feel ancient, as this channel only shows the old movie classics. Another special Beatles/John Lennon DVD I love and recommend highly is *Nowhere Boy*. This movie was especially impressive as it brought me back to Liverpool, Mendips, and the path of the very young lads that we, too, passed through during our 2012 visit. Seeing the inside of the childhood home of John Lennon at Mendips once again was cool as I was able to recall Aunt Mimi's kitchen and John's teeny tiny bedroom.

The sale of the Fab Four merchandising has gone through the roof worldwide, but especially in London and Liverpool. During my many trips there, there were endless items branded with the Beatles logo and I tried to really control myself, but had to give in to a few. A coffee mug here and there, an espresso cup as well, a picture calendar, a T-shirt, and a shot glass from the Cavern, and yes, all the other silly stuff. Silly, yet I still love seeing these things as I pass the day. The end game on all of this, though, is I have to stop somewhere. Who will want all my souvenir stuff and vintage memorabilia after I'm gone? Will anyone care or just throw these away? These thoughts are haunting. I fear the latter, but hoping the glory of the group will light up a little something in someone close to me and it all will live on. It has to. The longevity of fun I have experienced from the Beatles is meant to be shared. We all need a light to shine in our lives.

(I also have along with all Mrs. Harrison's saved letters a scrap of lined paper with the words below, written in blue ink:

To Lana

John Lennon.

I cannot verify if this is his actual signature, but it definitely came inside one of her letters one time or another. I do not recall anything more about this loose, lonely little piece of paper.)

Postmarked from WOOLTON, LIVERPOOL '25—31 AU 65

"I will be happy when they all arrive home safely."

Chapter 16

LATE LATE KARAOKE—PAUL MCCARTNEY— JUNE 2018

Well, tears were shed once again. Ok, I'm getting older and being overly sentimental has always been a part of me—all I need is a little something to set me off. These days, anything Beatles seems to easily do it, giving those heartstrings a little pull.

Watching *The Late Late Show with James Corden* and his Carpool Karaoke episode with Paul McCartney was a late-night snack I thoroughly enjoyed. Simply delish. It turned out to be very funny yet somewhat emotional. Corden seems to bring out the ultimate in his guests and this Karaoke sing-along was one of his best ever. Yes, I'm just a tad partial.

Sir Paul gave us a hint of a different look. It appeared he was starting to let us really settle in on his aging process. He had let his natural gray hair peek through all along his hairline and side-burns, which forced us to come to terms with yet another stage of our dear Paul, age seventy-six. The songs, though, were so Paul, so Beatles. In partic-ular, the *Let It Be* segment was thoroughly tearful, and I couldn't hold any back as I watched even James Corden get choked up.

Paul calmly explained, "…that's the power of music, it's weird isn't it, how that can do that to you." OMG, we get it, no worries, mate, we believe. We truly believe.

The car ride through Paul's hometown of Liverpool also hit a special spot in my heart as it brought me back to my 2012 trip. I viewed once again Penny Lane, St. Barnabas Church, the famous barber shop, and his family house at 20 Forthlin Road. These steps through his childhood home were intimate steps for me, too, as Paul guided the audience through the place I once walked, and as he played at the piano I remembered so well. I enjoyed how he spoke of his dad and mentioned a fun time with him while they still lived together in that house. It was during the period that Paul was getting quite famous and his dad always gave away his disguise when he was trying to escape the fans. His dad was fun-loving and would even invite the fans in for tea.

This reminded me of Mrs. Harrison and how she was much like Mr. McCartney. She was a loving, caring parent, making George's house a home, and she, too, enjoyed the fun of the fans. I was touched to read in one of her letters how she lovingly wrote, "I will be happy when they all arrive home safely." Yes, home, back in Liverpool with family; that was *home* for all of them.

The final scene of this special was at a local pub where they performed long ago, the Philharmonic Dining Hall; it was a fun mini concert and the cherry on the cake. There I was once again, watching people of all ages feel the rapture of the music, many with smiling, exuberant faces and many with tears of joy. There I was once again, enthralled in a Beatles melody of hits and emotion at a fever pitch. There I was once again *in heaven.* The show was another welcome break in my routine, and a *ticket to ride* to last a lifetime.

I was having a good time lately as specials like this and all those 50th Anniversaries of Beatles kept popping up. Those moments were filling all those empty nest Fab Four feelings that lay dormant on and off, giving me a reason to awaken them at any point in time.

Postmarked from WARRINGTON-LANCS. A.—12 JAN 1969

"We are about 250 miles from London about 4 1/2 hours drive, it's quite a long way."

Chapter 17

JUNE 1, 2019, DEADLINE—THE LAST HURRAH

June 1, 2019, was a date I thought would arrive someday, but always put in the back of my mind like that dentist appointment you wish will never come. When that day was approaching, it seemed more devastating than I would have liked to imagine. That was the day BA had calculated my flight benefits would end forever. When I received the letter from Staff Travel back in 2009 advising their revision to the benefits and telling me that my privileges would eventually have an end date, I thought to myself, "2019 is so far away, I have loads of time." Well even though I am not so naïve to understand and realize that time surely flies by awfully fast, it all came as a huge blow. Now I find myself upon that fateful day with *no loads of time left*. More than the full travel benefits being taken away, I feel like I've been sort of disowned by my family. BA had been my family since 1970 and I loved that feeling of belonging I could always count on. I was now hit with the uncomfortable sentiment of no longer being a part of the elite clique, the group, the airline staff comrades; I will become an outsider and it stinks! I always loved that sense of being in that private club of jetsetters, enjoying the same mind-set of my staff buddies who completely understood the trials and tribulations of standby travel, but appreciated the love of knowing the world in a unique way. It all has been a major part of my life and rather hard to actually let go. But, at the end of the day in all of this, the fact remains, no truer words will ever be uttered from my lips than, "I am forever grateful for the joys British Airways has given me."

As the June 1, 2019, date was approaching, I realized my last trip would have to be an especially memorable one, and the task at hand was to decide *where to?* I knew I wanted Liverpool in there somewhere, and I convinced a good buddy, Kathy, to come along for the ride. We decided, though, to add another country or two in the mix to make it a real send off. We would go to Switzerland, Southern Germany, and Lichtenstein before ending in London and Liverpool always in the hope this would be an epic "last hurrah."

Kathy, a Beatles fan, but not a classic Beatlemaniac, humored me and thought it would all be a zany, crazy fun time. Being a longtime airline employee, she had traveled to Liverpool a few years ago, but only for a day and not with the intensity of a trip with me. I mean, come on, the Beatles—Liverpool—me, I think she really didn't know what to expect. Well, we made it happen and off we went in early May. We would squeeze that last jaunt in just before the looming deadline. Typically, the flights were rather full out of JFK, but we managed to get on the third flight out that evening and with a little luck and help from the counter agent we got on Club Class. I was ecstatic. At first, I was trembling with fear that we wouldn't get on at all and to make it on Club was a nice touch. Not getting on would mean a disaster for the connecting flight to Zurich, but all went well and all without a hitch. We toured, bused, walked, munched, fondued, cocktailed, shopped, and photographed our way through many cities in Switzerland, the Alps, the land of Heidi, Bavaria's Black Forest, and the teeniest, tiniest country of Lichtenstein. We had our share of various types of weather: sunshine, clear and warm, cold, wind and rain, snow and cool crisp days. All experienced in the month of May, "quite unusual" as quoted by the local Swiss. We shared priceless laughs and created memories that will forever remain close to our hearts.

We were then ready for our London/Liverpool leg of the trip. Leaving Zurich in Club Class was a pleasurable detail and we landed at LHR quite early that morning. We then caught the bus into London Victoria Coach Station and had a few hours to kill before our five-hour journey to Liverpool. I had been to London with Kathy once before so we both were on familiar ground. We calmly stepped out of the bus, knowing exactly where we were and walked a few blocks to enjoy a cappuccino and cupcake at the "you know where" place. Yes, of course it was the lovely pastry shop, Peggy Porshen; we hadn't planned it, but things fell into place and we found ourselves enjoying a very special added moment.

Taking a bus to Liverpool was also not in the original itinerary, but in planning we learned on that day the Euston train station would be closed. Who closes a train station?!? We were gobsmacked to put it mildly, and the coach was our only means of transportation to Liverpool. So, bus it would be, and it actually turned out to be spectacular. Mrs. Harrison had described it in one of her letters as "a four-and-a-half-hour drive, it's quite a long way." She was right and it was taking the long way, but we had more than our share of beautiful English countryside and good weather along the route to enjoy. It turned out to be very relaxing and we had our chitchat time sharing Beatles stories. I was getting Kathy ready for Liverpool, until she finally said in amazement, "You could be on a trivia show about the Beatles; you know it all." We both laughed, and I especially got a kick out of her comment. Yes, I loved my Beatles, and I couldn't help myself sharing the joy.

We arrived at One Bus Station, Canning Place, in Liverpool and my immediate surroundings were all new to me. As we ventured off to find the direction we needed to be in, I realized it was beginning to look a bit familiar. I mentioned to Kathy, "Okay, I sort of remember this. There is Albert Dock." It was a very sweet recall. We kept walking and asked a few people the way to the Hard Days Night Hotel. Of course, I had to stay there again; I could not pass up that opportunity. Yes, and the people, oh, how I remember the people. Everyone being so friendly and just about becoming your new best buddies in only a few short moments seemed to bring back more familiar memories.

Each step you take, around every corner you turn sort of means something to a Beatlemaniac, and once there, you are utterly surrounded by the sensation of THEM. You know they walked these very streets all the time, and now we were here, too! The whole city embraces the memory of the Beatles as young lads just starting out. They love it as much as we do, and you get their euphoria if only in their friendly faces; the Liverpudlians are so proud of "the boys" and proud to be from Liverpool. The city had become even more scenic since the last time I was there. It actually had turned into a Fab Four Disneyland destination for Beatles people.

Suddenly, we turned a corner and there was the Hard Days Night Hotel in all its glory. We had made it to the hotel in no time at all. Liverpool proper is so small, everything is in walking distance to each other and the stroll through the streets was easy.

The hotel is a magnificent building, old world, stoic, and regal. Of course, regal, the Beatles are royalty after all. We did our check-in, gazed around, and I could tell Kathy was suddenly spellbound. I was reliving my first visit and about to be totally enthralled by my second. I couldn't be happier. As I walked around the lobby, I noticed that nothing had really changed. It was as breathtaking as I remembered it to be back in 2012. I had those butterflies flitting in my stomach once again and enjoyed the moment.

We were both super excited and super hungry, so we dropped our bags in our room and were soon out the door to find a fabulous pub for a traditional meal. On a recommendation from a local "Scouser" in one of our conversations getting directions, we were told of an area with nice pubs. ("Scouser" is derived from scouse which is a stew that was originally eaten by sailors and locals who worked down at the Merseyside docks. It is part of the Liverpool history and has also become a nickname for the dialect of English spoken in Liverpool; it is very much associated with the local Liverpudlians.)

After our quick few words with the local, we were off by foot to twist and turn from one road to another to find the area around Hope Street on the east side of town. This trip for me was about being in the total heart of Liverpool city. In 2012 with Deb, we did the fabulous tours to areas just outside Liverpool center. We encountered some hot spots on Matthew Street and Albert Dock, but never really explored the inner workings of the city. We had only two days and those tours Deb and I took were a must if it was to be the once-in-a-lifetime experience. I was never really sure if I'd return. Of course, I always wanted to, but never too sure if I could make it happen. With little time on my first trip, the childhood homes of John and Paul, 174 Mackets Lane, The Casbah Club, Penny Lane, and St. Peter's Church took top billing over anything else in center of Liverpool. But now, here I was indeed back again and in these upcoming two days with Kathy I would see the parts of Liverpool I missed the first time and get a real feel of the city. We would venture out and see all the city's nooks and crannies. I was, once again, *in heaven* in my faraway home.

We found a cozy pub, had a pint and a glorious meal of Fish and Chips. It was all so typical, but oh so good. We asked a few folks at the next table if there was any news about the royals and "the baby." We found out that Archie had been born that day to the Duke and Duchess of Sussex, and we were a bit elated. Kathy and I definitely felt a British sense of pride being there for the birth. So we all were dressed in our smiles.

Leaving the pub, we strolled our way back to Matthew Street for an evening at the Cavern Club. You certainly get that perky feeling once you enter; it is a classic music lover's fantasy escape. What I noticed is that you immediately realize that it's not just you, not just "people of your age," it is all ages, all shapes, and sizes. A crowd of people swinging, swaying, moving, and, dare I say it, "grooving" to some cover group or solo playing any Beatles song they can—everyone holding their iPhones up to record and saving their special memories of what they are witnessing. Everyone would want to be close to the Fab Four's spirit as much as humanly possible. The Beatles had certainly transcended in my lifetime to capture the minds and hearts of millions and millions of people, and I am not exaggerating in the least by that statement. We hung out for a while and thoroughly enjoyed the sounds and setting. We bought some "Cavern" souvenirs, and then headed back to the hotel. After our long day, we were ready to hit that comfy bed with the portrait of John Lennon in sunglasses and cap hanging over our heads. Bliss.

Next morning, we woke with huge plans for the day. We had to pack as much of Liverpool into this one day as we could. Leaving the next day on the 2:30 p.m. train back to London would give us very little time. We started with the traditional English breakfast in Blakes, the Hard Days Night Hotel's restaurant that Deb and I visited in 2012. The restaurant was named after Sir Peter Blake, British pop artist, who created the brilliant album cover for the *Sgt. Pepper's Lonely Hearts Club Band* LP. There was the spectacular buffet of breakfast foods to choose from and the huge collage of Sgt. Pepper's people on the wall to view. It was the perfect way to start our day.

First stop would be the Museum of Liverpool located at Pier Head, Liverpool Waterfront, to enjoy a free exhibit called "Double Fantasy." How fortunate we were to be in Liverpool during this gallery display that was planned to be there for just a few more months. Double Fantasy is the world's first show that portrayed John and Yoko's life story using many never-before-seen items from their private collection. The exhibit featured photographs, handwritten lyrics, and personal items, with music, film, and art created by both of them. It was a magical array of memorabilia that brought you even closer to John, Yoko, and yes, you couldn't help but be drawn to the aura of the Beatles as well. It was, though, strictly a John and Yoko show with many expressions of their love and devotion to each other. It also highlighted their passion for the continuing Imagine Peace movement. While there, Kathy and I posted notes on the Wish Trees and Remember Love wall that were featured there. After the closing of the exhibition,

all notes and tags were to be stored at the Imagine
Peace Tower, Yoko's memorial to John, which she
unveiled in 2007 on the Videy Island, Reykjavik in
Iceland. How cool is that? We even posted a note for
our Beatles buddy, Debbie, as she was with us on this
journey in spirit.

Next on our itinerary was to find the newly created
bronze statues of the Fab Four situated in front of
the Cunard Building and just outside the Beatles
Story's Pier Head site. The beginnings of the statues came from Chris Butler, Managing Director of
Castle Fine Art Foundry Ltd, and donated to the city
by the famous Cavern Club. The statues of the lads
stand tall in their exquisite bronze glory which was
beautifully and artfully created by sculptor Andy
Edwards; he captured perfectly the immediate recog-
nizable images of the young Fab Four. It is definitely a place of reverence that one can visit to
reflect and adorn.

Once Kathy and I found our way to the site, we
were in seventh heaven. It was a spectacular monu-
ment and we were mesmerized by this beautiful tribute to them. We were surrounded by many football
fans from Barcelona who were in the city to watch
the UEFA Champions League semifinal match between
Liverpool and Barcelona being played that night at
Anfield. The Barcelona fans took a number of photos
standing in front of the statues with their city's
logo banners and scarves all eager for the upcoming
game. We waited our turn and snapped as many photos
as we could together in front of the statues, alone
in front of the statues, and then just the magnificent statues solo. Being witness to this amazing
work of art one can understand why it brings so much

pride and joy to the people of Liverpool and ultimately the world. We also suddenly remembered the
James Corden Carpool Karaoke episode that featured
some fans taking pictures in front of the statues, and how surprised they were to discover Paul
McCartney peeking out from behind them. As we stood
there, we kept looking around with just a glimmer
of hope Paul might pop up again somehow somewhere.
Yes, a mere glimmer.

We continued our way through the Albert Dock
area, hitting a few souvenir shops and gazing at
the calm and splendid Mersey River. The afternoon
would start with lunch at the Philharmonic Dining
Hall, home of the mini concert performed by Paul and
shown on TV during the Carpool Karaoke special. We
entered and bellied up to the bar, ordered our meal
of a typical meat pie with veggies and a pint. We
then walked through the short hallway and found our
way to the dining room to sit. It was fun to reminisce those moments of the show and have lunch at a
table that was situated right in front of the large
window and makeshift stage where our beloved Paul
stood and sang.

Then we were off to find the Jacaranda Club, which
was pretty much up there on the list of sights and
landmarks in Liverpool for Beatles fans. Located on
Slater Street, we mapped our way through the area
and finally found it. Only one little glitch, it was
closed. As we tried moving the door and mentally beg,
"Please be open," a gentleman out front was talking
to a few people and took notice. He happened to be
the manager and could see we were desperate to check
out the inside. He unlocked the door and nicely gave
us our own private mini tour. We were under that

Beatles lucky star yet again and enjoyed the sweet kindness of another fab Liverpudlian.

The Jacaranda was another home of the Beatles and has been an important part of the Liverpool music history since 1958. The club was frequented by "the boys" and was a special hangout for Stuart Sutcliff (original Beatle). Some of Stuart's artwork has been restored and is still hanging there. The club is located near the Liverpool Art College that John and Stuart attended and is close to the Liverpool Institute attended by Paul and George. In 1960, the five founding members of the Beatles, called the Silver Beetles at that time, staged some of their earliest public performances in the basement of the Jacaranda and appeared there just before their trip to Hamburg. In his mini tour, our courteous friend brought us down to the area where they performed. It was significant and I had a Casbah moment remember-ing those very beginnings. This is where they started their professional career with their first manager, Allan Williams, who happened to be a co-owner of the club. It was another milestone and key point for the band. The club was named "Pubs in Time" in February 2006, and it is still open to musical groups performing in the same room the Beatles played. The Jacaranda is also the home of a restored 1948 Voice-O-Graph booth (a machine that allows customers to make their own recording and press it directly to vinyl). This Voice-O-Graph happens to be one of the three remaining booths in the world open to the public. The Jacaranda is a major Beatles landmark, very much off the usual beaten Fab Four path of the famous Matthew Street, but worth the venture into a different part of Liverpool. It is certainly a recommended Beatles fan delight to discover.

We realized it was getting late in the afternoon and we still needed to find the Empire Theatre, which was the last venue the Beatles performed at as a group in Liverpool, and the Liverpool Town Hall where the Beatles stood on the balcony to 20,000 fans gathered to welcome them back to their native city in July of 1964.

Writing about our attempt to locate the Empire Theatre brought to mind a funny story. Kathy and I were wandering the streets and thought we were finally in the right area, but weren't quite sure. The Empire Theatre was pretty famous, but for a Beatles fan it had its own special significance. I decided to scope out an older person to ask directions, thinking that person would know exactly what I was talking about. We saw a group of street workers more or less our age and thought *these guys should know*. I approached one and started out by saying, "I need to ask you something as you are more or less my age—" and he interrupted me with an instantaneous comeback, "Why? Do you want to get married?" We all burst out laughing. I do so love Liverpool. The people are tremendous fun. Their humor is quick and often surprising. I always enjoyed "the boys'" charismatic wit and surely understand it must be a Liverpool thing—totally brill. We joked around a little with these guys and finally got directions to The Empire. One of them actually just about guided us the whole way; he was so kind. Once there, we took our photo of the theatre for posterity and headed out. Our funny encounter with the workmen, though, left more of an impression on us than the Empire

Theatre. We continually laughed all afternoon just thinking of it.

On our way toward the Town Hall, we noticed a Forever 21 shop at 12-14 Whitechapel. Remembering some trivia, it was the location of the legendary NEMS (North East Music Stores), which was run by the Beatles' famous manager, Brian Epstein. Also, NEMS was the place where Freda Kelly worked as Mr. Epstein's secretary. "The boys" were always there in those early days discussing business deals with Brian and just hanging out with *Good Ol' Freda*. She was one of the very original Beatles fans, and often during her lunchtime break she would pop over to the Cavern Club to watch them perform. NEMS was situated in proximity to Matthew Street, so it was an easy dash there and back to the office. Now, sadly though, this building is a Forever 21 clothing store and the memory of this musical landmark is just that, a memory. To my mind it was still noteworthy enough to photograph the Whitechapel sign at the very least because it will *forever* be a Beatles memory.

We finally reached the Liverpool Town Hall and the view was especially important as I recall many vintage black-and-white photos taken on July 10, 1964, of the lads on that balcony of the Town Hall. They had returned to Liverpool for a civic reception and for the northern premier of their first film, *A Hard Day's Night*. They enjoyed the chaos of the crowd and stood there looking at what was the frenzy to be for the rest of their lives. It was an unforgettable moment in Beatles history and another must-see for any avid Beatles fan.

We knew we had to squeeze in a visit to the newly opened Magical Beatles Museum located on Matthew Street and squeeze it in fast as they were going to close at 5:00 p.m. Rushing through the streets, we finally reached the Magical Beatles Museum (located at 23 Matthew Street) at 4:30 p.m. and pleaded to be let in even though we knew it would be a shortened tour. We met with Tom, and he guided us through the three floors of artifacts that would forever take our breath away. We started on the top floor with the history of the early Beatles and the story of the Casbah Club and the Best family. Information rarely portrayed (if only at the Casbah itself), but made its way to this museum courtesy of Roag Best, youngest brother of Pete. Nice. Tom went on about the details of those early years, which I knew from my tour of the Casbah back in 2012 with Rory Best, but all new for Kathy.

Tom was young, I'd say in his early twenties, but well read about Beatles and Beatles facts. I was impressed. At one point, though, I did get him to take notice when we passed a display of two red stadium seats that were donated by two Americans. They were two seats from the 1965 Beatles Concert at Shea Stadium. I questioned Tom about those "red seats" as I did not remember any seats being that red. I told him I was at the concert, and I thought I knew all the colors of the different levels of seats. His eyes opened wide, "You were there?!?" He was flabbergasted. I was an antique in full view, an actual live relic of that day in 1965. Those seats did throw me, though. I thought they must have been special box seats, and surely only a few as the red color never really stood out in the massive seating of 56,000. After that moment, he was our new best buddy and gave a more upfront and personal feel to the tour. We loved every minute. We saw many of the over 300 rare and authentic artifacts along with those red stadium seats. The majority of the antiques were behind their own cubed glassed enclosure. Items like John's harmonica used in 1966, John's famous round-wired eyeglasses worn circa 1967, the actual handwritten lyrics to *Lucy in the Sky with Diamonds*, real props used in the *Help!* movie, John Lennon's Sgt. Pepper Medals worn on his costume, the white cello highlighted in their *Blue Jay Way* music video, George Harrison's Futurama Grazioso guitar, and a small case used by George during 1963. His guitar leads were kept inside the case along with the settings for his amp which were written on the inside lid. There was also a guitar strap of George's that was used in 1963. There were lots of microphones, Paul McCartney's bass speaker from 1961 along with Pete Best's drum kit circa 1960-1962 used during their Hamburg days. A fountain pen that belonged to Brian Epstein and used by him at his office at NEMS was also prominently displayed. There was even an actual brick from the original Cavern Club. We also observed the penknife used by John Lennon to carve *JOHN IM BACK* into the red ceiling above the stage at the Casbah Coffee Club. As described on the sign beneath the display, the story goes—"When noticed by Mona she confiscated John's knife as it wasn't the first time he'd done something like this in her club." I remember well seeing his handiwork during my 2012 visit to the Casbah. There were also two German police "mug" shots of McCartney, P. and Best, P. taken upon their arrest in Hamburg for a minor incident of setting a small fire with a condom ☺. "Boys will be boys." This magnificent display of Beatles memorabilia was extensive and unequalled. I kept taking picture after picture for my travel album. I highly recommend a visit and totally agree with the sign outside the front door, "Roll Up, Roll Up for the History Tour." It is definitely a fab fun time.

After our tour, we made our way back onto Matthew Street to go to The Grapes and take a photo in the pub of each of us sitting in the exact bench seat as the Beatles sat during their early days. We also needed to take a photo next to the new bronze statue of Cilla Black situated outside the Cavern Club at 8 Matthew Street. Cilla was special to the Cavern as she performed there in the early '60s. She also worked there part-time as a cloakroom attendant. She was close friends with the Fab Four and was eventually discovered and managed by Brian Epstein, too. She was famous in her own right, and I recall adoring her and her style. I loved to copy the way she wore her hair. Her short bob was something I could slightly manage when I did my best to straighten out my curly locks before I grew it long. She was a pal of the Beatles, and I liked getting to know about the people that surrounded them and whom they liked.

We also stopped in the Cavern Club to book a tour next morning of the Beatles homes and sights outside of the city. I had done this before, but something new for Kathy. I didn't have to be asked twice to do a rerun of these historic places. I was totally onboard to enjoy it all a second time around. It was a perfect way to pass our morning and tie up all the loose ends of our wonderful Beatles experience.

Time was passing and getting into early evening. We decided we would venture out to a local pub to watch the Liverpool/Barcelona football match that evening at 8:00 p.m. We started chatting up with the doorman at the Hard Days Night Hotel, and he recommended a nice pub close by called Thomas Rigby's to enjoy the game.

We freshened up in our room, made some phone calls, and were ready to walk a few blocks to the pub. Before we left, I made another quick call to my son, Daniel, to let him know we were going to see the game at a local pub. He, too, was getting ready to watch the game but on TV in his home in Charlotte, North Carolina. Granted, we would be watching it on TV as well, but he knew watching it in a pub in Liverpool was an experience we wouldn't soon forget. He was thrilled, and we were getting a little excited, too.

Rigby's was established in 1726 and boasts as one of Liverpool's oldest and best loved pubs. We found it very inviting with lovely large white-paned windows all in a row, black wrought iron gaslight-look lamp out in front, and beautiful old-world oak and stained-glass door. We felt the quaint authentic 18th-century Britain vibe even before we entered. We arrived a few minutes into the game, but walked in at the most perfect moment. Goooooooooooooooooooal. We were caught up in the pandemonium the very second we set foot in the place, and we cheered and screamed along with the pub fans. I felt like we brought them luck as they all turned and smiled at us. The craziness had just begun. The Liverpool team was not expected to beat Barcelona, but beat them they did—4 Nil, and we became die-hard Liverpool football fans from that night on. Kathy had never even watched a soccer game before but was now in the know. We quickly made friends with the local fans which added to the fun. Thomas Rigby's was first-rate and we were so glad we took the doorman's advice.

After the game, we left the pub and walked the quiet streets in the direction of our hotel. Everyone in the city was either at Anfield Stadium or in their homes or at other pubs reliving the match and celebrating the victory. A homeless man sitting on the sidewalk shouted out to us, "You girls better get inside, this place is going to be nuts in about an hour." That is what Liverpool is all about; the kindness of the people never ends. He was looking out for us and we felt his sweet concern. We smiled all the way back to the hotel.

This city had a real home sentiment for me. I now became an adoptive daughter of Liverpool, and I would declare it to be one of my favorite of places I have visited. Since it was my second go-around of the area, I felt rather comfortable. I was now secretly a Liverpudlian and it was a happening totally due to my love for the city and the Beatles.

Next day, it was another fabulous breakfast in Blakes and off to the Albert Dock for our scheduled 10:00 a.m.-12:00 noon Magical Mystery Tour sponsored by the Cavern Club. Once we boarded the bus, it was pure excitement. The tour would take us by the childhood homes of the Beatles, schools, and art colleges, and get us up close and personal to some places that inspired some of their songs, Penny Lane and Strawberry Fields Forever. We passed by the childhood homes of Cynthia Lennon and Brian Epstein, something I didn't expect. Then the tour brought us right around an area I read about, but never thought to investigate. It was a bit of a surprise and a new sight to see and remember. There we were at the childhood home of George Harrison, 12 Arnold Grove, in the Liverpool suburb of Wavertree. This was pretty touching, as George for me was "the man" and I enjoyed seeing more of his history. I had only visited his Mackets Lane address back in 2012; I had been more interested in that home because of my letters. This Arnold Grove house, though, was especially famous as it was his birthplace. Much more has been written about this home than any other of his childhood residences. It was described as two rooms up and two rooms down, no central heating, and an outside toilet in the back. The very stark and humble beginnings of the Harrison household were here, and our young George lived in that house until he was six years old, but the rest of the family had lived there for twenty years.

So, this tour created a new memory for me and turned out to be a special send-off for our Liverpool escapade. We finished near the Cavern Club, which was close to our hotel. We checked out of our lovely Hard Days Night sojourn and were off to Lime Street station for the train ride back to London. Oh dear, goodbye sweet Liverpool.

The train ride was quick and painless, and we arrived safely at Euston station back in London. We walked to King's Cross station, took the train to LHR, and ended the trek at the Sofitel as I had done before, though never with such a heavy heart. A deep sigh seemed to make its presence; it was an emptiness that surrounded my being. These were the anxious and uncomfortable butterflies I was feeling now. It was all going to be over very soon, and I didn't like it one iota. I guess I could return, but the likelihood of these special scenarios through BA would be gone for good.

We enjoyed a nice meal and a restful night. We were up early next day and off to do my *last* BA employee check-in. There was that heaviness again. We were fortunate enough to enjoy Club Class on this last ride, and once AGAIN I was super thankful for all that had been awarded to me. Those BOAC/BA trips gave me lasting memories to keep close to my heart.

I will always love the nostalgic jolt I get when I see a vintage photo of the Fab Four disembarking an aircraft and seeing the BOAC logo on the plane behind them or when they are strolling along with their BOAC flight bag in hand. Those flights must have been lively and crazy fun. Imagine sitting in the row behind them or just being on the same plane? What a sweet ride that would have been!

I have a fun memory of a time when the Beatles were making a quick stopover at JFK International Airport via BOAC during the mid '60s. Jane and I made our way to the airport that afternoon in hopes of seeing them. We reached the International Arrivals Building (IAB), found the direction to the observation deck and joined the many Beatles fans crammed together in anticipation of something. We never actually saw them, but knew the air was filled with Beatles delirium. Among the many girls having an attack of the screaming meemies, we fit right in. Excitedly, I held my camera in the air and snapped a quick pic of the plane and crowd of people on the tarmac near the bottom of the staircase. We couldn't tell if they were in that crowd or still on the plane, but my very vague photo was my personal reminder of a Beatles/ BOAC moment.

Reminiscing now, though, I realize that I was in sync early on with my Beatles/BOAC/BA connection and the emotional spirit of my path in life. Being a part of the BOAC/BA family, I inherited my forever link to England. Even though it was a sad end to my special British Airways feel through travel, it could never be an end to my British feel through life. I discovered over the years my escapes to England were the most efficacious ways of awakening the heart and lifting the soul. England and the Beatles will continue to reign through. They are so a part of each other, and I feel extremely favored to be touched by both in an intimate way.

Postmarked from WARRINGTON, LANCS. D—13 DEC 1967

*"I have another grandson "Ian" Peter & Paulines
1st Baby."*

Chapter 18

NOT AN ENDING

———————

All generations think that their earlier times were
simpler, easier, and sweeter, and I cannot deny these
thoughts rest with me. I am realizing, though, some
things somehow come right around again. What's old
is new once more. The Beatles continue to be rele-
vant in this modern day. Their music is remastered
and now sold on vinyl LPs again. With the updated
versions and my vintage lot, I find myself now trying
to buy a decent record player. Paul and Ringo keep
creating so there is definitely very original material out there to enjoy, but still the Beatles' "old"
and classic stuff is very popular. They continue to

reinvent themselves, as well as the methods used to market them keep getting reinvented. In any case, they are all around, in many forms, attracting all ages to their distinction.

In present day, Sal and I are no longer together; both of us are experiencing new and different paths, but stay connected for our family. I have come to learn that he had recently traveled to London on a European vacation, and ever since his return, I noticed all three of our grandchildren wearing beautiful Beatles T-shirts from Nonno. Isn't that something? Even though we may not be together, it seems the memory and glory of the Fab Four is forever, and my zany infatuation became a part of Sal and our children.

I fully intend to continue my fun and introduce the reality of the Beatles and their sounds to my grandchildren. How cool it would be to swap grandma stories with Mrs. Harrison's. I am sure her grandson, Ian, was a joy for her and Mr. Harrison as she mentioned him often in her letters. Sadly, she only had a short time to be with him. It is a little crazy now when I realize and think Ian would be a grown man in his fifties by now.

My grandson, Alessandro, is well on his way to learning and knowing what the Fab Four are all about as he readily calls out each of them by name when looking at their photos. He loves to sing along to *Yellow Submarine* while performing the ritual wave with those little fingers in the "peace" style formation. Even sweet little granddaughter Sophia swings and sways her body to the famous Ringo tune, an entertaining song for both of them. The song

Blackbird also has some hypnotic hold on her as she sings it constantly. She also adores the John Lennon solo *Julia* as it reminds her of her new baby sister, Giulia. Of course, granddaughter Giulia will also be Beatles-enlightened when the time is right. All aboard the Beatles train, my little cherubs. I hope they all will someday enjoy reading this and realize with great surprise that their Grandma had a lot of fun. Maybe someday they will even visit Liverpool and remember my story, which may bring a gentle smile on their faces.

As I call to mind those early years, this fun I was able to acquire had much to do with my parents. It could not have been possible if I was not a product of a loving and supportive home. Thoughts and thanks are always in my heart for dear Mom and Dad. They let me be as excited and enchanted as I wanted to be; they let me enjoy those blissful days and brief period of delightful weather. In my case, it was all about these Beatles. To the average outsider, it was a silly thing, but for a young teen in the sixties, it was a biggie.

I have to laugh when I think about the very beginnings of the Beatles and all the critics saying "they will never last." How comical this sounds now. Their music, their personalities, their greatness have become everlasting to everyone and, happily, to me as well. I even feel a bit proud. I say a bit because these were not my Beatles; yet in a selfish way they were mine to me. I was pleased to have gotten it right. These guys were brilliant and knowing that I understood this from the start gave me that bit of personal satisfaction.

Even though I do realize I am a neophyte story-teller, writing this memoir has brought me much joy. I've had a happy time thinking back and reliving those special series of Beatles-inspired events. Writing it all down keeps these sentiments fresh and forever. I do admit it all seems rather odd that as a grown "older" woman I could still get so stirred up about them, but there you have it. It is what it is. Happiness is definitely a prize many of us are lucky enough to come by, and the Beatles have always been my ongoing "jackpot" through the years.

I probably should be quasi winding down on this personal Beatles saga, but strangely enough, I feel there is more in store for me. I would like to think I will get back to Liverpool once again someday, who knows. I recently learned of a new project in the works, The George Harrison Woodland Walk Memorial due to open in 2021 in Allerton, South Liverpool. The 12-acre green area will combine garden and wood-land with many artistic installations that symbol-ize George's life and lyrics. It sounds wonderfully inspirational and a perfect excuse to make that return trip.

Debbie and I will continue to remember their style and enjoy whatever is new and exciting with the Fab Four. Yes, new and exciting regarding a musical group that I have enjoyed and grown with for well over fifty years. Thinking about those words, "well over fifty years," sounds much too old, but in my heart and soul, I'm simply and yet still, just a girl who *loves* the Beatles.

EPILOGUE

Recently after my flight from Palm Beach, Florida, to Charlotte, North Carolina, landed and I was in the gradual taxi to the gate, I reached down at my feet, grabbed my old classic navy canvas BOAC/BA flight bag, and placed it on my lap. This bag is something I enjoy using on my travels. I am a fan of the unusual and this personal item has vintage distinction. Soon, I am sure, it will have vintage extinction. I can catch one on eBay now and again, but they are becoming increasingly rare.

While I was mentally getting myself ready for that mad dash off the plane, a gentleman one row back and across the aisle reached out, tapped my bag with his finger, and said, "Nice, I like your bag." I thanked him and then went on to explain how I used to work for BOAC when the merger with British European Airways took place and that's how BOAC is the BA of today. He knew all about the history and couldn't wait to remind me that BOAC was mentioned in the Beatles' song *Back in the U.S.S.R.* I felt a bit of a smirk coming on and thought—*Hello, sir, are you speaking my language?* Of course, the brief conversation went into the Fab Four and quick mentions of "remember when" continued. Our rows were up, and we were on our way to squeezing through the carry-ons and the other passengers. As I went out in front of him, I left with a smile, a wave, and a "nice talking Beatles with you, have a great day." There could never be an end to any of this; it all continues to live on forever because I keep it close in mind and heart as I have always done. I have an ever-loving connection; I am a lucky girl.

ACKNOWLEDGMENTS

A big thank-you and hug to Debbie for the guidance and support I needed to get me through the baby steps of this huge undertaking. She was with me at the beginning and stayed strong through the rest. This also holds true for our longevity as pals. Most importantly, I want to give thanks for her loving and comforting friendship and sisterhood after all these years.

A resounding applause to Janis for her patience and expertise in putting me in directions I never knew I could go as a writer. Her critique was every-thing I needed to keep this going in those new ways I had to explore and she guided me through the process. I love her closing remark after each email, "Be inspired in Love and Light." I am forever thankful for her kindness and encouragement.

To all my girlies, Christina, Claudia, Jaymi, Kathy, Lesley, Liliana, Linda, Lynda, and Valerie—a special thanks for the once and twice-overs in the early draft days. I surely needed their perspectives to move me along and keep me going and growing with confidence. Happy thoughts and gratitude to Jane; it was a thrill to have her review our fun times of those beginning Beatles years. Fact is, you always need your girlies, and I love them all.

I was interested in a man's opinion, so my brother was commissioned to have a read-through. Also, as he is somewhat part of my story and craziness, I thought I'd better give him a heads-up. Thanks go out to Joe and his wife Vivian for their comments and morale-boosting.

Then there is Maria—from her genuine enthusiasm of my idea of this manuscript to her immediate proposal announcing she would do the cover artwork, I am forever grateful. Her love and support have always carried me along, and her artistic talent is more than evident. I appreciate her assistance and skillfulness in organizing my thoughts for my photo *anthology* collage.